How to Discipline
Your Child

(Without Going to Jail)

Alan M. Davick, M.D.

How to Discipline Your Child
(Without Going to Jail)
Alan M. Davick, M.D.

ISBN: 978-0-9890053-6-4

MISKIDDING, LLC
P.O. Box 101127
Cape Coral, FL 33910-1127
URL: www.DrDavick.com
Email: miskidding1@gmail.com

Cover Photograph: © Stephen Denness | Dreamstime.com
Cover Design: Rik@PublishingSuccessOnline.com

DISCLAIMER

This book is intended to be a guide to disciplining children. It is not intended to be a recipe for diagnosing or treating physical or mental illness, nor does the purchase of this book establish in any way a professional relationship with the author or publisher.

The author and publisher are not responsible for the use or non-use of any diagnostic procedure, treatment option or choice of medication mentioned in this book. The reader is cautioned new information regarding diagnostic procedures, treatment options and medication-related information accumulates daily and may render the examples presented in this book outdated or even contraindicated by the date of publication. Therefore, the author and publisher do not assume and hereby disclaim any liability to any party for any loss, damage or disruption caused by error or omission in this book and associated websites or videos.

This book and associated websites and videos are not intended to replace medical, neurological, genetic, psychological or psychiatric advice tendered by the reader's own professional consultant(s) and the reader is strongly advised to discuss any pending decisions regarding diagnosis, treatment options or medication with such consultants.

Scenarios presented in this book as examples of discipline are completely fictional and none of the characters, names or scenarios are drawn from factual case histories. They represent brief summaries of the author's experiences over many years and any similarities between the characters portrayed or examples given and actual case histories are purely coincidental.

Acknowledgments

The principles presented in this book are distilled from the *MIS*/Kidding® **Process**, published separately in **Managing Misbehavior in Kids: The *MIS*/Kidding® Process** and were developed by the author over many years with the painstaking collection of expertise from colleagues in the fields of Medicine, Psychology and Education as well as from interaction with innumerable families. A mere listing of all those who influenced this effort would fill many books this size!

The author must mention his gratitude to Rik Feeney, author, editor, publisher and coach, whose unfailing professionalism and ready advice has made the writing of this book and its predecessors a pleasure.

And, yet again, to my wife, Barbara, whose patience seems limitless!

Al Davick

Table of Contents

Preface

Parents *can* go to jail for disciplining their children.

Most people now define discipline as the imposition of punishment to insure the following of rules. For example, in my child psychiatric practice, parents typically view discipline much as it's currently defined online at *Merriam-Webster.com*[1]:

: control that is gained by requiring that rules or orders be obeyed and punishing bad behavior

: a way of behaving that shows a willingness to obey rules or orders

: behavior that is judged by how well it follows a set of rules or orders

Note the first and most usual definition ending with: <u>punishing bad behavior</u>.

But discipline in the hands of parents is better defined and more effective when older, perhaps even obsolete definitions are employed. Here's how discipline was defined in Webster's New Universal Unabridged Dictionary in its 1979 edition[2]:

:training that develops self-control, character or orderliness or efficiency

Employing this definition of discipline enables parents to achieve loftier goals than the mere following of rules. While police officers, temporary caretakers and substitute teachers might restrict discipline to compliance with rules, parents' goals include their children's attainment of adulthood and, hopefully, independent life.

With today's focus on punishment rather than the development of self-control, character, orderliness and efficiency, it's not hard to see how the line between instruction and abuse can become a matter of opinion – often a child's opinion. While our society has focused disciplinary efforts on punishment, it has encouraged our children to interpret almost any punishment as abuse. Indeed, our children have now become empowered to report *their* concept of abuse to law enforcement agencies, who in turn assume parents guilty of abuse till proven otherwise. These days, parents *can* go to jail for disciplining their children.

This book takes an instructional view of discipline. If you're a parent, the simple techniques presented herein will transport your children from "can't" to "can" and from "won't" to "will" while developing self-control, character and responsibility. Used as directed, these strategies rarely cause the anger that fuels reports of abuse. Nonetheless, the disciplinary models you will learn from this book are even more powerful than traditional forms of punishment.

References:

1. "Discipline." *Merriam-Webster.com.* Merriam-Webster, n.d. Web. 4 Apr. 2014. <http://www.merriam-webster.com/dictionary/discipline>.

2. Webster's New Universal Unabridged Dictionary, Deluxe Second Edition, Dorset & Baber, 1979.

Introduction

In the Preface, I mentioned how the concept of discipline has changed over the years from a means of instruction to a means of ensuring compliance with rules. With that change has come a reliance on punishment. All psychiatrists and most parents know that punishment often leads to anger and/or depression. Anger creates defiance and sometimes outwardly directed violence while depression often immobilizes the recipient and may lead to self-injurious behaviors.

As a parent, why choose, at the very least, to add to the burden of child-rearing by creating anger, with resultant defiance and possibly outwardly threatening behaviors (even homicide), or depression with potentially self-injurious behaviors (even suicide)? Can we do better than relying on punishment, with its potential hazards (even jail), to impose discipline? The answer is both yes and no. Yes, in that powerful rewards can be used to motivate better choice-making. No, in that failing to earn such powerful rewards is itself a form of punishment. But failure to attain rewards, rather than leading to anger with its hazardous consequences, most often creates disappointment or guilt – both useful instructional tools for children, though often disparaged by the politically correct.

In the chapters that follow, we'll explore the use of rewards for appropriate behavior. Not just any rewards, but rewards so powerful and compelling that not earning them is sufficient to overwhelm traditional punishment, while earning them propels children toward adulthood.

In looking for rewards to safely and effectively discipline children, we'll need to choose rewards that meet certain criteria:

• They must be at least as powerful as punishments.

•Parents must "own" them. That is, they must be rewards parents can give their children at will, but which their children cannot take from parents unless they are given.

•They must be affordable, even for the most financially challenged family.

•They must carry little risk of creating anger or depression.

•They must be perceived by children as rewards under all circumstances.

•They cannot be bribes.

Before we go further, let's deal with two misconceptions parents often rely upon when they hear the word "reward," especially when speaking of rewarding "good" behavior. The first misconception is created by confusion over the difference between rewards and bribes. The second misconception is a child should not have to be rewarded to do the right thing.

What's the difference between rewards and bribes?

Rewards are desirable consequences earned by expending efforts toward achieving defined or required goals. Because they are consequences, rewards always follow efforts (acts), or achievements. Children (and adults) who have earned rewards for efforts or achievements are motivated to earn more rewards for such efforts or achievements. By using rewards to energize discipline, we'll be encouraging children to earn more rewards by continuing to expend efforts on right acts. We'll examine the use of rewards in the next paragraph, but first, let's distinguish rewards from bribes.

Rewards given before they are earned are bribes. Parents who use bribes to discipline children are presenting the children with a mere wish for good behavior. Since bribes are rewards given before they are earned, they pose no risk of ill consequences to children who choose to misbehave. Bribes are a form of dishonest communication conveying the message that lack of effort or achievement will be rewarded. Even if parents follow such a formula, the rest of the world won't. Bribes are always an inappropriate and ineffective tool for encouraging right behavior.

Why should parents reward children for doing what is right?

This is a very important question because the answer leads parents to a better understanding of parental objectives and children's motivations.

We'll begin to answer this question by stating that, with only two exceptions, everyone acts (behaves) the way they do for a reason. This includes children. The two exceptions are psychotic individuals (crazy people) and sick people. Psychotic people are often defined as individuals who cannot link their acts to the consequences of their acts (e.g. – complaining of police following them while walking around naked). Likewise, physically ill people often have little or no direct control over their symptoms (e.g. - epileptics having seizures).

The reason all people who are neither psychotic nor sick do what they do is they anticipate desirable (from their viewpoint, of course) consequences. And, as we'll soon see, the quest for desirable consequences is the foundation of effective discipline.

As children grow up, what they perceive as "right" is built on an ever expanding collection of desirable consequences for having acted correctly. The younger the child and the fewer the desirable consequences the child has experienced for choosing right, the less committed the child will be to performing such acts. A parent's role is to build for their child a compelling collection of consequences for doing right. Since children enter the world without any pre-existing consequences, parents must provide such in the form of rewards for choosing to do right. Expecting children to choose right over wrong for no reason is truly expecting psychotic behavior from children.

OK, we now understand why discipline relying upon rewards is better than that employing punishment; we can avoid creating anger or depression. Since we don't expect psychotic behavior from our children, we'll reward them for choosing to perform right acts. And, we no longer confuse rewards (consequences) with bribes (rewards given before they're earned).

This is a good place to ask: What are parents for? That is, what's the ultimate goal of parenthood? Is it merely to ensure the following of rules till a child reaches 18 years of age? Is it solely to receive the love and affection of a younger generation?

I believe the overriding goal of parenthood is the molding of children into adults. I don't believe adulthood has a set age. Rather, adulthood is best defined, in my opinion, by individuals' readiness, willingness and capacity to accept responsibility for the consequences of all their acts. By this definition, it's easy to see how some right acting children may be given adult responsibilities and privileges while some adults who are unwilling or unable to engage in right acts, would never be entrusted with the same.

So, if parents are charged with the job of transforming children into adults by creating in them the readiness, willingness and capacity to accept responsibility for their acts, it will be through instructional modes of discipline that this process will be achieved. These disciplinary modes must use powerful rewards as consequences for right acts, giving children good reason to make right choices and so encouraging them to accept greater and greater responsibility for their acts.

Now we're ready to move on and see how it's done. Before we begin, let's visit the *Glossary* and glance at a few terms you'll soon be encountering. Don't try memorizing them! They'll all be explained later and in more detail.

Glossary of Terms

Discipline:A changing concept. It's presented in this book as an instructional process for children, encouraging right acts and leading to adulthood through acceptance of responsibility.

•**Word language:**Spoken language, often directed at children to guide them away from misbehavior and toward right acts. Such language expresses mere wishes and is typically ignored unless it is honestly and consistently linked to consequences.

•**Action language:** Actions or events that communicate to children.

•**Action language consequences:** Actions or events, which when linked as consequences to word language, create disciplinary commands.

•**Discipline commands:** Powerful forms of discipline in which word language is linked to action language in the form of rewards or punishments. Four disciplinary models are presented in this book. Each model is expressed verbally then "energized" with consequences:

o**Brick Wall model:** A word language command using punishment(s) alone to stop misbehavior.

o**Billiard model:** A word language command presenting punishment(s) to redirect misbehavior while offering reward(s) to encourage right acts.

o**Distraction model:**A word language command presenting two or more rewards together to distract a child from misbehavior and encourage right acts.

o*Hansel & Gretel model:* A word language command presenting two or more rewards, one after another, to lure a child to right acts.

Right acting behavior: Constructive behavior moving children along the path to adulthood. Such behavior supports growth in the physical, social, and communication skill areas of Age Work, good relationships with Others, and acceptance of reasonable rules from Authorities.

Misbehavior: Undesirable behavior. It's defined by its effects on children or adults, specifically, by threats to the Consequence Areas. Misbehavior slows or blocks progress toward adulthood.

•*Annoying (trivial) misbehavior:* Behavior causing minimal emotional reaction by observer(s) and little or no threat to the Consequence Areas. This behavior scores 1-2 points on the misbehavior scale. Discipline is squandered on this behavior and it is best ignored.

•*Moderate misbehavior:* Behavior scoring 3-6 points on the misbehavior scale. This level allows time for discovering underlying causes and developing strategies to manage it.

•*SEVERE misbehavior*: Misbehavior intense enough to threaten a life-endangering outcome and which, in the case of children, requires a person in authority to stop it with whatever degree of force is needed. Such misbehavior leaves no time for discipline or the development of management strategies until it has been lessened to a moderate or lower level. It generates scores of 7-9 points on the misbehavior scale.

•*Defiant misbehavior:* Willful misbehavior causing significant threats to Consequence Areas and causing moderate emotional reactions by observers. This misbehavior allows time to develop management strategies and responds to discipline once underlying physical or mental disorders have been eliminated or accommodated.

o*Active defiance:* Children choosing to do things they should not do.

o*Passive defiance:* Children choosing not to do things they should be doing.

• *"Hardwired" misbehavior:* Misbehavior caused by physical or mental health disorders which take away children's choice-making abilities. Hardwired misbehavior cannot respond to discipline.

• *Complex misbehavior:* Misbehavior exhibiting both willful defiance and an underlying physical or mental disorder.

Consequence Areas: Areas of critical life functions for children threatened by and used to define misbehavior.

• *Age Work:* A Consequence Area comprised of physical, social, and communication skills children must attain at each stage of life to function normally. Successful achievement of Age Work depends upon a child's healthy body and mind. Deficiencies in any of the following fields of Age Work may be caused by or may create misbehavior.

o*physical:* The field of Age Work comprised of organ and muscle-related capabilities, including stamina, dependent on a healthy body.

o*social:* The field of Age Work relying on mental health and expressed by interactive skills enabling children to enjoy and benefit from being with others.

o*communication:* The field of Age Work comprised of language-based skills, which includes academic performance.

• *Others:* A Consequence Area encompassing a child's interaction with all others. Failure of acceptance by or complaints from others are a measure of misbehavior.

•*Authority:* A Consequence Area defined by a child's relationship to people in charge, such as parents and teachers. Right acting behavior requires the acceptance and following of reasonable rules. Inability to follow reasonable rules is a measure of misbehavior.

Misbehavior Scores: Sum of points generated by misbehavior. Points are assigned for the number of observed threats to critical life functions and for the intensity of emotions experienced by observers.

•*Objective scores:* Points assigned to the number of observed ill effects of misbehavior on the Consequence Areas of Age Work, Others and Authority.

•*Subjective scores:* Points assigned to the intensity of emotional reactions experienced by observers of misbehavior.

o Merely annoying misbehavior generates total scores of 1-2 points.

o Moderately intense misbehavior is defined by scores of 3-6 points.

o SEVERE, life-endangering misbehavior generates scores of 7-9 points.

• *Misbehavior Scale:* A simple way to rate the intensity of misbehavior.

Consequences: Events triggered by children's behavior or misbehavior which may occur spontaneously or which may be devised to redirect children's behavior.

• *Rewards:* Pleasant consequences for right acting behavior.

• *Bribes:* Rewards dishonestly offered before they've been earned.

• *Punishments:* Painful or unpleasant consequences. Though efficient in stopping misbehavior, they do not promote right acts and often provoke anger or depression.

HoNoR Role: A model parents can use to grow children into adults, consisting of Honesty, Nurturance and Responsibility.

•*Honesty:* Keeping spoken commands consistent with predicted consequences.

•*Nurturance:* A supportive relationship between a child and an adult comprised of love and affection. As a consequence of behavior, nurturance is a powerful source of motivation for converting misbehavior into right acting behavior.

o*Love:* A series of supportive acts, offered as a heritage and never dependent upon good behavior.

o*Affection:* A demonstration of liking and acceptance which can and should be made dependent upon right acting behavior and which may be offered as a reward for right acts.

o*Superaffection:* Affection created within a loving relationship (as with parents). More powerful than affection outside a love relationship (as with babysitters).

•*Responsibility:* The characteristic which distinguishes children from adults. Children who are ready, able and willing to accept responsibility for all their acts have become adults.

Professionals: People with special knowledge about children and their misbehavior who can help parents with difficult disciplinary problems, especially "hardwired" conditions.

•*Physicians:* Medical doctors who examine and treat children with physical problems by doing lab tests, prescribing medicines, doing surgery or hospitalizing children.

•*Psychologists:* Professionals who can measure intelligence and assess emotion using standardized tests and who can provide counseling and psychotherapy.

•*Educators:* Professionals primarily concerned with academic performance and who have access to special schools and educational services.

"Parents teach children discipline for two different, indeed diametrically opposed reasons: to render the child submissive to them and to make the child independent of them. Only a self-disciplined person can be obedient; and only such a person can be autonomous." —Thomas Stephen Szasz

Chapter One

Does your child need to be disciplined?

None of us, psychiatrists included, have enough energy or time to monitor and redirect all the things children do each day. If we are to use discipline to guide children to perform right acts, we'll need to limit our efforts to behaviors truly worthy of our time, attention, and efforts. To get the job done we need to answer three questions:

- What's misbehavior?

- What's right acting behavior?

- When is misbehavior severe enough to require discipline?

What is misbehavior?

In this book, I define misbehavior from a parent's perspective. Baby-sitters and other temporary guardians view misbehavior differently from parents. Merely annoying behavior may trigger discipline from non-parents. But from a parent's view, trivial misbehavior having no impact on certain life functions we'll soon define are best ignored and are unworthy of discipline.

Look at this list of misbehaviors:

- A baby crying for a bottle at night

- Overeating and under-eating

- Refusing to give up the bottle

- Playing with fire

- Smearing spaghetti in hair

•Hitting brother on the head with a bottle

•Biting teachers

•Writing on walls with lipstick

•Failing in school

•Not making friends

•Breaking rules of courtesy

•Drug abuse

•Sexual promiscuity

•Attempting suicide

We recognize each of these as misbehavior and know that each must be controlled. Intuitively, we also know some of these misbehaviors are more serious than others. In the next chapter we'll see how to rank them by their seriousness and, by so doing, determine how best to manage them.

So, how do we know the examples listed above are misbehavior? We recognize them as misbehavior by looking at their effects. We look at the consequences of suspicious behavior to decide if it's misbehavior.

The consequences of misbehavior, depending on their duration and intensity, interfere with a child's attainment of adulthood and independence and, if severe enough, can lead to death. Behaviors having no recognizable consequences are unworthy of discipline and should be ignored.

An easy way to check the consequences of misbehavior

We can organize our thinking about the consequences of misbehavior if we imagine misbehavior targeting three critical life functions. Most important and central to right acting behavior is a child's physical and mental health. Next in importance is a child's ability to coexist peacefully with others. Finally, a child's ability (or inability) to follow reasonable rules determines that child's safety and degree of independence from the direct control of authorities (such as parents, principals, policemen.)

As we observe the consequences of a child's behavior in order to identify misbehavior, it's useful to visualize the relative importance of each of the three life functions of physical and mental health, reactions of others and effects on authority.

Let's call all the skills that depend upon normal physical and mental health at each age, Age Work. The effects of behavior (or misbehavior) on people coming in contact with a child we'll call Others. A child's ability to abide by reasonable rules we'll call Authority.

Misbehavior can be recognized by its injurious effects on Age Work, Others and Authority. Right acting behavior grows a child's competence in these three Consequence Areas.

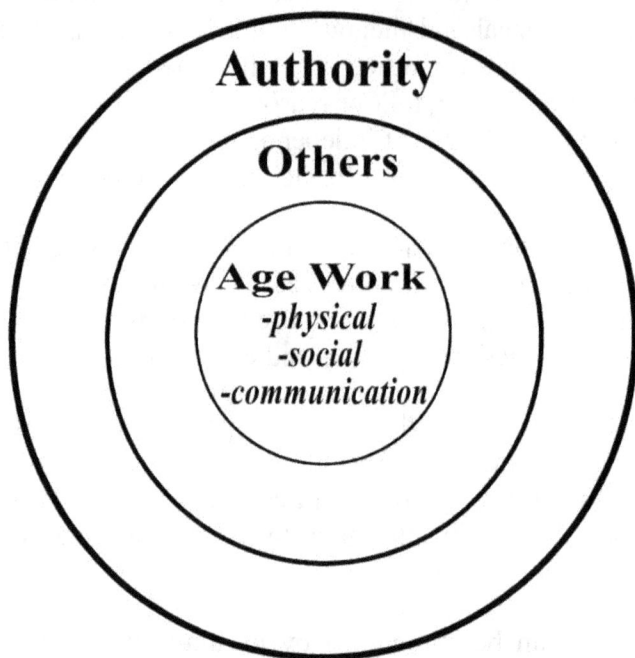

The Consequence Areas: Age Work, Others, & Authority

The consequences of misbehavior target Age Work, effects on Others, and effects on Authority – the Consequence Areas. Let's take a closer look at these skill areas.

•**Age Work** consists of the body and brain skills children must attain at their various ages. For example, normal one-year-old children should be able to walk, smile at their parents with recognition and use single words. In this example, and in all age groups up through the teen years, *physical, social* and *communication* skills like these are expected by certain ages. Delays in Age Work can be either a cause or an effect of misbehavior. For example, a teenager who cannot maintain grade-level work in school may choose to be truant (a case of misbehavior causing academic failure), but might suffer from learning disabilities (in which delays in communication skills create the appearance of misbehavior.)

Age Work is the easiest Consequence Area to measure because professionals have studied and published normal expectations for physical, social, and communication skills for each age. A table of normal skills for each of the subcategories of Age Work is presented in Appendix I.

•**Others** consists of the effects of misbehavior on Others, including people at home and out of the home. These effects can be observed by parents, but are often reported by the Others themselves. Complaints from Others as a pattern of behavior qualifies as misbehavior.

Judging misbehavior by its effects on or complaints from Others is less exact than that of Age Work, though when large numbers of complaints are generated there is little doubt of misbehavior.

•**Authority** consists of compliance with reasonable rules. Failure to comply with reasonable rules, used as a measure of misbehavior, varies in definition from one household to another and from one authority to another. For this reason, used alone as a measure of misbehavior, threats to authority are a weaker indicator of misbehavior than are effects on Age Work or Others.

Using the Consequence Areas as measures of misbehavior

I've placed Age Work at the center of the Consequence Areas because delays in any of the areas of physical, social, or communication skills are most often due to medical, psychiatric, or genetic abnormalities over which children have no direct control. Some of the causes of these delays can be increasingly destructive to brain or bodily functions over time (like tumors, some forms of epilepsy, lead poisoning, and many others).

•The physical subcategory of Age Work is comprised of organ (including brain) and muscle-related capabilities, including stamina and is dependent on a healthy body.

•The social subcategory of Age Work encompasses interactive skills enabling children to enjoy and benefit from being with others. These skills also depend upon a healthy body and mind.

•The communication subcategory of Age Work includes all the means by which academic functioning is expressed. This skill area, too, depends upon a healthy body and mind.

How "Hard-Wired" Misbehavior differs from Defiant Misbehavior

I call misbehavior caused by disturbances in any of these divisions of Age Work, over which children have little or no direct control, "hard-wired" misbehavior. Threats to Age Work are often caused by hard-wired disorders. Unlike misbehavior targeting Others or Authority, threats to Age Work are rarely due to acts of defiance and such misbehavior, from a parent's view, rises above the level of mere annoyance.

The more outward placement of Others as a Consequence Area and an indicator of misbehavior reflects the personal and emotional nature of complaints from others. Unlike Age Work, for which professionals have established norms, the thresholds for complaints from Others vary from one person to another. Still, counting complaints from Others can be quite a revealing measure of a child's misbehavior.

Threats to Authority are placed in the outermost position of our diagram of the Consequence Areas because some authorities are stricter than others and the definition of reasonable rules varies from one authority to another and from one family to another. The importance of threats to authority also varies with the power of an authority. For example, the significance of threats by a younger brother to an older brother's authority would likely fall well below threats by that child to the authority of his parents or a policeman.

When misbehavior affects Age Work, hard-wired disturbances are at play; that is, there's an underlying disorder of body or mind

24

affecting Age Work. By contrast, misbehavior only affecting Others or Authority, without any any disturbance of Age Work, is always due to willful defiance.

Let's look at a few examples of the Consequence Areas as measures of misbehavior. We'll begin with Age Work, the innermost realm of Consequence Areas. Remember, you can check the expected Age Work for a child of any age in Appendix I.

Using Age Work to test for misbehavior in an elementary schooler

Elementary schoolers are expected to go to school unless they are ill. They're expected to be able to use a pencil, attend to their bathroom needs, and communicate with their teachers. If an elementary schooler cannot hold a pencil, wets or soils his pants repeatedly, or doesn't speak to his teachers, he's misbehaving in the realm of Age Work.

- *physical*: Can't hold a pencil; wets or soils clothes

- *communication*: Doesn't speak to teachers

Using Age Work to test for misbehavior in an adolescent

Adolescents are expected to keep friendships (without relying on unlawful activities, like drug abuse or drunk driving). They should be able to participate in physical education activities at school and maintain their grades in the range of their abilities. Deteriorating stamina or coordination, losing friends, or suddenly falling grades are examples of misbehavior within the realm of Age Work:

- *physical*: Deteriorating stamina or coordination

- *social*: Losing friends

- *communication:* Falling grades

25

Now we'll look at effects on Others, a second realm within the Consequence Areas, as a tool to recognize misbehavior. We'll use an infant as an example to demonstrate the use of this Consequence Area as a measure of misbehavior. Effects of misbehavior on Others apply equally well to all age ranges.

Using effects on Others as a measure of misbehavior in an infant

How children get along with Others around them is determined both by the quality of their behavior and by Others' reactions to it. Disturbing those around them as a pattern of behavior qualifies as misbehavior. Parents must take note of Others' reactions to their children's behavior.

Though some parents may not mind babies crying through the night to be fed or held, visitors to their home may feel otherwise. When babysitters, relatives or the grandparents sleep over, objections may be raised.

●Others: Household guests complaining about baby crying.

Whether or not parents see this behavior as unacceptable for their baby, the effect of the behavior on Others is decided by the Others. Parents who accept babies crying all night can prevent this from becoming misbehavior only by avoiding ill consequences to Others. When Others are in the picture, *they* decide whether they have been targeted by misbehavior. Of course, Others can decide, too, that babies crying all night do not distress them.

The last Consequence Area we'll examine is effects on Authority. Normal behavior in this realm is characterized by children's ability to accept and abide by reasonable rules. Misbehavior is defined by breaking reasonable rules.

Here's an example of effects on Authority as a measure of misbehavior in a toddler:

Using effects on authority to define misbehavior in a toddler

Toddlers occasionally resort to biting their caretakers and other children. This usually occurs during temper tantrums and is not otherwise frequently seen. Sometimes temper tantrums and biting are a child's preferred response to the setting of limits. When this becomes a pattern of response to Authority, it becomes misbehavior.

●Authority: Toddler biting another child or adult.

I've met parents who accept being bitten by their children. If they are their children's sole targets and don't consider their Authority threatened, the test of Authority is passed. But if their children bite Others, or the parents do consider their Authority threatened, misbehavior is defined.

Is there a SIMPLE way to use the Consequence Areas to identify misbehavior? Yes, indeed!

Whenever you suspect misbehavior, ask yourself:

●Is your child showing deficiencies in Age Work?

oBody or mind? (*physical)*

oRelationships? (*social*)

oAchievement / Schoolwork /(*communication*)

●Are Others complaining about your child?

●Are reasonable rules being broken? (Authority)

Besides observing the effects of suspect behavior on Consequence Areas to identify misbehavior, our emotional reactions provide a second valuable measure of misbehavior.

How our emotional responses help define misbehavior

Think about the last time you watched children misbehaving. Depending on what you saw, you probably experienced one or more of the following emotions:

annoyance - mild reaction

Confusion / Anxiety / Anger - Moderate reactions

FEAR - INTENSE reaction

Parents experience a mild emotional reaction of annoyance when they encounter unpleasant behavior they've seen before, but from which they anticipate no ill effects to the child or anyone else in the near future. In other words, they just don't like it!

Confusion, anxiety or anger as emotional responses to misbehavior are moderately intense reactions. Misbehavior causing such moderate reactions causes parents, either consciously or unconsciously, to suspect or recognize troublesome outcomes for the child, for themselves or for others.

Confusion or anxiety is generated when the cause of misbehavior is unclear to parents. These emotions are sometimes created by threats to Age Work and their presence suggests the behaviors may not be under the child's control.

Anger, also a moderately intense emotional reaction, is generated when parents realize behavior is calculated by a child to force them to accept consequences they don't want to accept or to do things they don't want to do. This emotional reaction is a reliable indicator of a child's willful defiance.

FEAR is, of course, a severe emotional reaction to the recognition of a likely and immediate threat to someone's wellbeing – either the child's or someone else's.

In the following table, I've grouped the misbehaviors listed earlier in this chapter, linking the severity of each to typical emotional reactions described by parents. The emotional reactions generated in observers are arranged into three categories – mild, moderate or severe. Though parents may each have somewhat different responses to any of the behaviors, it's rare in my experience for parents to assign any of the behaviors to an altogether different category.

Severity	Examples of Misbehavior	Emotional Response
SEVERE	Toddler playing with fire Adolescent attempting suicide Toddler hitting brother with a bottle Elementary schooler abusing drugs Adolescent engaging in sexual promiscuity	FEAR
Moderate	A baby crying round the clock Failing in school Not making friends and losing old ones Overeating and under eating	Anxiety
	Biting the nursery school teacher Writing on walls with lipstick Smearing spaghetti in hair Being discourteous	Anger
	Refusing to give up the bottle Baby crying for bottle at night soon after last feed	Confusion
mild	Refusing to hug or kiss Mommy Not finishing a meal Saying, "You're a bad Mommy (or Daddy)!"	annoyance

Categorizing emotional responses to misbehavior

Parents are remarkably consistent in describing their reactions to misbehavior. Within the Moderate group, one parent may be anxious while another is confused, but few parents disagree enough on their emotional reaction to choose a wholly different category.

Why is it important to judge the severity of misbehavior?

Determining the severity of misbehavior allows us to save our energy by safely ignoring mild misbehavior. Recognizing SEVERE misbehavior prompts us to STOP it however we must before taking time to impose discipline. And limiting discipline to misbehavior in the Moderate category allows us time to develop and apply selected models of discipline.

In the next chapter, we'll see how we can combine effects of misbehavior on Age Work, Others, and Authority with a rating of the emotional reaction the misbehavior creates. By combining effects on the Consequence Areas with a guesstimate of our feelings we'll be able to place any misbehavior in its category of severity and, by so doing, decide how to manage it.

The Permissive Idiocy: *Kids have the right to do as they please and the world must adapt to their misbehavior.**

*Adapted from Managing Misbehavior in Kids: The *MIS/*Kidding® Process *by* Alan M. Davick, M.D., MIS/KIDDING, LLC, 2014

Chapter Two

Is there time for discipline?

In the last chapter, we saw how threats to Age Work, Others, and Authority as well as the intensity of our emotional reactions to suspect behavior can be used to identify misbehavior.

We learned severe misbehavior, threatening injury or even death in the short term, must be STOPPED immediately with overwhelming force if necessary. Such misbehavior leaves no time for parents to discover causes or to apply discipline.

We also learned moderate misbehavior needs to be controlled, but does leave time to search for causes and apply discipline. By forcibly stopping and eliminating severe forms of misbehavior and ignoring mild misbehavior, we can limit our disciplinary efforts to moderate misbehavior and allow ourselves time to determine causes and develop strategies.

A useful scoring system to categorize misbehavior

I've found it useful to use a simple scoring system to categorize misbehavior. This scoring system is valuable because not all severe, potentially, life-threatening misbehavior creates fear on the part of parents in its early stages. If we are to recognize severe misbehavior in its earliest stages, we cannot rely entirely on intuition. Another value of this system is its ability to define trivial misbehavior, reassuring us we may safely ignore it.

In the last chapter, we learned how to use both observed threats to Consequence Areas as well as our emotional responses to children's behavior to identify misbehavior. Now we'll assign scores of intensity to our observations and our emotional responses. By combining these objective and subjective scores, we'll be able to

31

safely categorize misbehaviors and so determine our best course of action.

Scoring observed (objective) effects of misbehavior on Consequence Areas

The effects of misbehavior on Consequence Areas may be assigned levels of severity. In this diagram from Chapter One, I've scored threats to each of the Consequence Areas.

Age Work: You already know the skill areas of Age Work, *physical, social,* and *communication* depend upon a child's healthy body and mind. This means misbehavior flowing from or affecting these areas could be inherited or due to a physical handicap or mental illness. Such misbehavior, not under a child's control, cannot respond to discipline.

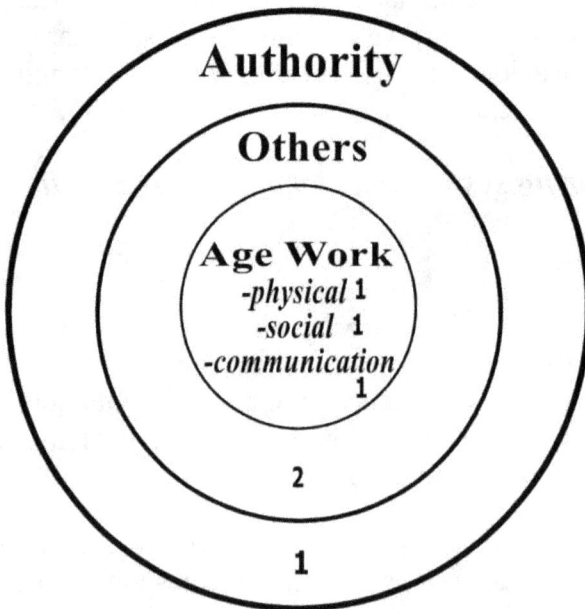

Failure to achieve Age Work is easily recognized (and norms are simply presented in Appendix I). In this scoring system, each affected component of Age Work (*physical, social,* and *communication*) is assigned a point score of 1 for a maximum of 3 for threats to Age Work.

Others: There are two groups of Others who may be affected by misbehavior; parents and everybody else. I've assigned a score of 1 to parents and another 1 to everybody else. Misbehavior affecting Others may generate up to 2 points.

Authority: The interpretation of misbehavior affecting Authority rests heavily on opinion and varies widely from one authority to another. For this reason, I've assigned the Consequence Area of threats to Authority only 1 point.

Here's a summary of the scoring of observed effects of misbehavior on Consequence Areas:

Age Work
 physical   = 1 point
 social   = 1 point Total: 3 points
 communication = 1 point
Others   = 2 points
Authority   = 1 point

As you can see, if all the Consequence Areas were to be threatened by a child's misbehavior, the highest observable score would be 6 points. We may call points generated by effects on Consequence Areas an objective score.

Now let's examine our emotional response to misbehavior, the second part of the scoring system. We may call points generated by our emotional reaction to misbehavior a subjective score.

Scoring emotional (subjective) reactions to misbehavior

Based on many years of observation, I've assigned the following scores to the emotional reactions of observers of misbehavior. If several observers (like two parents) are reacting to a behavior, I score only the single most intense reaction.

Here you see the highest possible score generated by your emotional reaction to a misbehavior is 3 points.

annoyance = 1 point

$$\left.\begin{array}{l}\textit{Anxiety}\\ \textit{Anger}\\ \textit{Confusion}\end{array}\right\} = 2 \text{ points}$$

FEAR = 3 points

A score of intensity of a misbehavior is like degrees of heat on a thermometer. The greater the heat, the more dangerous the outcome. As parents, our job when we encounter misbehavior will be to "cool" intense misbehavior to safe and manageable levels.

We may combine the scores generated from our observations of misbehavior and its effect on Consequence Areas with that generated by our emotional reaction to the misbehavior. This provides an accurate measure of its severity and potential danger.

Here's how the combined scores of any misbehavior, translated into degrees, can be used to construct a Misbehavior Thermometer. The thermometer allows us to recognize and eliminate severe misbehavior, ignore trivial annoyances and devote our efforts to disciplining moderate misbehavior.

A Misbehavior Thermometer: Using the Scoring System

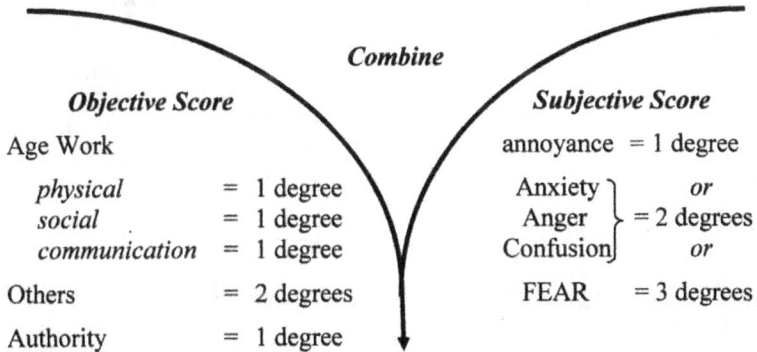

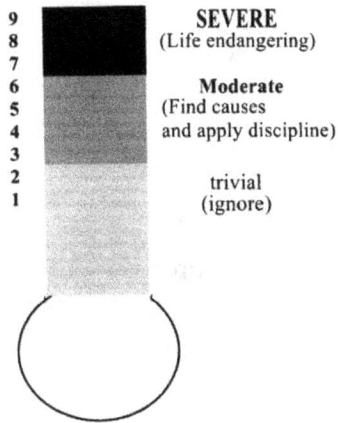

Combine

Objective Score

Age Work

physical	=	1 degree
social	=	1 degree
communication	=	1 degree

Others = 2 degrees

Authority = 1 degree

Subjective Score

annoyance = 1 degree

Anxiety ⎤
Anger ⎬ = 2 degrees
Confusion ⎦

or

or

FEAR = 3 degrees

9	**SEVERE**
8	(Life endangering)
7	
6	**Moderate**
5	(Find causes
4	and apply discipline)
3	
2	trivial
1	(ignore)

The simplest way to use the scoring system is to imagine a Misbehavior Thermometer, such as is shown above. Scoring ranges for severe, moderate and trivial misbehavior can easily be envisioned. The scores shown combine the observed effects of misbehavior on Consequence Areas with the observers' most intense emotional reaction to the misbehavior.

Scores between 7 and 9 define severe misbehavior, leaving no time for exploring causes or applying discipline. Such misbehavior must be stopped immediately, using whatever (legal) means are required. Scores of 3, 4, 5, or 6 represent moderate misbehavior which leaves time for determining causes and applying discipline.

Scores of 1 or 2 define trivial misbehavior, which may safely be ignored.

SEVERE Misbehavior: Turn down the heat immediately!

Scores of 7 through 9 on the thermometer define severe, potentially life endangering misbehavior. The value of the scoring system is highlighted by the fact many parents don't recognize this level of threat till disaster has actually occurred. By using this scoring system parents can identify misbehavior which will lead to severe outcomes *before* children or those around them suffer harm or even death.

In situations where children may attempt suicide, for example, the misbehavior score will rise into the severe range long before any physical threat is seen. These scores identify deadly misbehavior *early*.

The appropriate response to severe misbehavior is always immediate action to "cool" it to a lower level of misbehavior. Such intervention *is not negotiable* and should not be influenced by a child's preference to avoid controlling the misbehavior.

When life or limb is threatened, *overwhelming force may be necessary* to control the misbehavior. Before I show you how to use overwhelming force legally and effectively, let's see some examples of how the scoring system is used to identify and distinguish the various categories of misbehavior.

Identifying severe misbehavior

Scores of 7-9 on the thermometer are the result of threats to all three areas of Age Work (3 degrees), plus complaints from Others (parent[s] and anyone else = 2) and at least a Moderate (2 degrees) emotional reaction by observers. Many variations are possible, but severe misbehavior is accurately defined with a score of 7 or more. This is so even if FEAR is not the most intense emotion experienced by the observers. Since most parents don't recognize severe misbehavior until or unless it creates fear, this scoring system is most useful in identifying severe misbehavior at its beginnings and prompting intervention *before* injury or death occur.

We'll begin with some intuitively scary behaviors which cause fear in the typical observer, then follow with less obvious, but equally dangerous behaviors which parents often allow to continue at great peril.

Examples of severe misbehavior generating scores of 7-9

These are scary & usually recognized as severe misbehavior:

Misbehavior	Observed °'s	Emotion °'s	Total
A baby choking and blue	**Age Work** = 3 Threat to all 3 skill areas **Others** Parents & family = 2	**FEAR=3**	**8**
A toddler jumping in front of a car	**Age Work** = 3 Threat to all 3 skill areas **Others** = 2 Parents & family	**FEAR=3**	**8**
Attempted suicide by a teenager	**Age Work** = 3 Threat to all 3 skill areas **Others** = 2 Parents & family	**FEAR=3**	**8**

These are less often recognized as severe, life endangering misbehavior:

A four year old biting anyone who approaches & mutilating herself; spoken language limited to single words	**Age Work** = 3 Threat to all 3 skill areas **Others** = 2 Bites parents & others **Authority** = 1 Breaking rules	Anxiety=2	**8**

Misbehavior	Observed °'s	Emotion °'s	Total
A teenager losing friends, always tired, falling grades	**Age Work** = 3 Threats to all 3 skill areas **Others** = 2 Parents, teachers voicing concern	Anxiety=2	7

38

Now we've learned to recognize severe misbehavior and understand if it's ignored it may lead to catastrophe, let's see how we can best STOP severe misbehavior. Our goal is to convert severe misbehavior into a less intense or even trivial form of behavior which we can take time to assess, discipline, or even ignore.

How to convert severe misbehavior to a lesser level

Here are the examples of severe misbehavior you saw above. Each of them generated 7-8 degrees on the scoring thermometer:

- A baby choking and blue

- A toddler jumping in front of a car

- Attempted suicide by a teenager

- A four year old biting people, mutilating herself, using only single words

- A teenager losing friends, always tired, with falling grades in school

In each situation, threats to the physical, social and communication skill areas of Age Work contribute 3 degrees. For these examples, the fastest way to convert severe misbehavior to a lower level is to remove the threats to Age Work. Removing points generated by threats to a child's physical, social and communication skills lowers the score by at least 3 degrees and transforms the severe misbehavior to a moderate level (7-9 degrees become 4-6 degrees).

For the baby, clearing the airway, giving CPR, if necessary and getting medical help removes the threats to physical, social and communication performance, the foundation skills of Age Work. For the toddler, forcefully removing the child from danger eliminates such threats as well. For the suicidal teen, the teen who is always tired, losing friends and failing at school and for the four-year-old girl who is biting, mutilating herself, and failing to exhibit skills expected for her age, professional help will be needed to remove the children from immediate danger. To a geneticist or neurologist, the four-year-old girl mutilating herself might arouse suspicion of a progressive, brain-damaging condition. To a psychiatrist, the suicidal teen might be suspected of suffering severe depression with the possibility of suicidal acts. To an endocrinologist or oncologist the teenager always feeling tired, failing in school and losing friends might suggest hormone deficiency or leukemia, respectively. The point is, many possible conditions might be at play for any of these children. But as a parent, you need make no diagnosis other than severe misbehavior to take action. Once severe misbehavior has been identified, you must forcefully remove your child from danger, either yourself or with the assistance of an appropriate professional, including on occasion, a policeman. Recalling severe misbehavior can result in death to a child or others, hospitalization, when proposed by an appropriate professional, must be considered *non-negotiable*. A 911 call is often required for a combative teenager faced with hospitalization.

In the next chapter I'll show you how to choose the most appropriate professional to recognize and manage misbehavior due to underlying problems over which children have no direct control. First, let's look at a few examples of merely annoying misbehavior as defined by the scoring system. Disciplining this level of misbehavior, in my opinion, is a waste of your time and energy.

Using the Misbehavior Scale to define Trivial Misbehavior

Though children are "out of control" when they engage in merely annoying misbehavior, the only Consequence Area typically affected is Authority (generating 1 degree) and the only typical reaction generated in the observer is annoyance (1 degree). If any more degrees result from the behavior, as for example with Authority (1 degree) and Anger (2 degrees), the misbehavior has intensified to a moderate range and will require discipline.

Here are two examples of merely annoying (trivial) misbehavior:

Example of Trivial Misbehavior	Observed °'s	Emotion °'s	Total
A toddler saying, "Daddy, I hate you," after being denied dessert.	Authority = 1	annoying=1	2
Example of Trivial Misbehavior	Observed °'s	Emotion °'s	Total
An elementary schooler crying for Mommy after being put to bed	(no consequences) = 0	annoying=1	1

Can we really ignore merely Annoying (trivial) Misbehavior?

Observing annoying misbehavior is a very personal experience for a parent. After all, no one else suffers any consequences. Because parents have only so much energy to spend on disciplining their children, it's best to avoid imposing rules if those rules aren't worth enforcing. Disciplining merely annoying misbehavior is a luxury parents can't afford.

Here are some rules I've seen parents use to justify disciplining a child. If breaking these rules generates only 1 or 2 degrees on the misbehavior scale, the misbehavior is defined as merely annoying. See if you don't agree with me you've got better things to do with your time and energy than enforcing such trivial rules as these:

Infancy

•Take as much formula from Daddy as from Mommy.

•Don't cry when you see Grandma. Stop throwing your pacifier on the floor.

Toddlerhood

•Stop asking me to read a story after you go to bed.

•Stop sucking your thumb.

•Don't touch your (genitals – bellybutton – nose...)

Preschooler

•Stop wetting the bed at night.

•Eat your green vegetables.

•Stop breath holding when you cry.

Elementary schooler

•Stop masturbating in your room.

•Stop complaining about the clothes I select for you.

•Make your bed as carefully as I do.

Adolescence

• Don't waste your allowance on toys.

• I don't care about the other kids, dress the way I tell you.

• Do your homework as soon as you get home from school.

Any of these behaviors can eventually graduate to more than mere annoyance. If they continue long enough or begin to affect Others or even begin to disrupt a child's physical, social or communication skills (Age Work), the misbehavior will generate a higher score. Scores of 3-6 points leave the merely annoying category behind and enter the moderate range.

In this chapter, I've shown you examples of severe misbehavior and merely annoying misbehavior. What remains after merely annoying and severe misbehaviors are eliminated is moderate misbehavior. I've purposely omitted examples of moderate misbehavior from this chapter. The remainder of this book focuses on identifying the causes of moderate misbehavior, choosing disciplinary models to redirect it and energizing those forms of discipline.

Once you've "cooled" severe misbehavior to a moderate or lower level and recognized and decided to ignore merely annoying misbehavior, you'll have time to determine whether the remaining moderate misbehavior can respond to discipline or whether physical or mental disorders are present which prevent your child from acting right.

Before we proceed to Chapter Three, where we learn when to suspect misbehavior children cannot control and how to choose professionals to identify and manage the causes of such misbehavior, let's apply all we've learned to two more complicated, but realistic examples.

Converting Complex Misbehavior to a moderate or lower level

Two Preschoolers

Tommy and Bobby, aged three years, are playing near an open window in a third story apartment. Tommy suddenly stands and throws a metal matchbox car out the window and watches it smash on the ground. His friend Bobby climbs onto the windowsill to see more clearly. Mom turns and sees the boys.

Terrified, she grabs Bobby by the arm and yanks him to the floor. Bobby shrieks with fright, while Tommy screams, "Bad Mommy!" For several hours afterward, Tommy refuses to hug Mommy.

Discussion: Mommy recognizes Bobby on the windowsill as severe misbehavior and stops it immediately by physically removing him from danger. She ignores the boys' immediate reactions of crying and screaming at her as examples of merely annoying misbehavior. Tommy's refusal to hug her, another example of merely annoying misbehavior, is also ignored. If it were to persist, it would eventually become moderate misbehavior and require management.

An Adolescent

Janet, 16 years of age, is seeing Hugh, 24-years-old. She is failing her major subjects and her parents discover she has missed two weeks of school. Janet has been caught selling marijuana at school. Court action is pending. When her parents attempt to ground Janet to the home to stop her from seeing Hugh, she threatens to run away or take an overdose of pills. She claims if her parents loved her, they would trust her and let her see Hugh.

With the advice and support of their pediatrician, the parents arrange for Janet's immediate admission to a secure adolescent psychiatric facility.

Discussion: Janet taking and selling drugs as well as her threat to overdose on pills generate scores of severe misbehavior. Her parents decide to stop the life endangering threat immediately by arranging a secure psychiatric hospital admission. Applying the scoring system you've learned to Janet's failing grades, playing hooky from school, and the relationship with Hugh, the parents recognize each behavior as moderate misbehavior. As such, each misbehavior will require intervention, but there is time for discipline later. Janet's claims of not being loved and trusted are examples of merely annoying misbehavior and can be ignored. If they persist long enough to rise to a level of moderate level, they will also require parental action.

If, in attempting to stop Janet's illegal selling of drugs and get treatment for her suicidal thinking (both forms of severe misbehavior), Janet were to rebel against hospitalization or attempt to run away, it would be appropriate to *forcefully restrain her and hospitalize her against her will.* This would most likely require a 911 call.

Once we recognize misbehavior, determine its intensity and "cool" severe misbehavior to a moderate or lower level, we'll be left with moderate misbehavior which may or may not be responsive to discipline. Our next step is to identify and either manage or accommodate any underlying physical or mental disorders contributing to the misbehavior, but which are not under the child's control. This is important because such conditions, when mistaken for willful defiance, don't respond to discipline.

The Protective Idiocy: *Kids are too frail to accept the consequences of their acts and too dumb to learn from them.* [*]

[*]Adapted from Managing Misbehavior in Kids: The *MIS/*Kidding[®] Alan M. Davick, M.D., MIS/KIDDING, LLC, 2014

Chapter Three

Recognizing & managing "hardwired" misbehavior

I've chosen the phrase hardwired misbehavior to describe misbehavior caused or influenced by underlying physical or mental health conditions over which children have no direct control. These physical or mental conditions may take away from children their ability to choose right from wrong behavior. Children who are not free to choose right from wrong cannot respond to discipline. Indeed, disciplining children who suffer from such conditions creates anger or depression, intensifying the misbehavior.

Events happening within children over which they have no control all find their roots within the skill areas of Age Work. That is, hardwired misbehavior is expressed through faulty physical, social, and communication activities.

Typical causes of hardwired misbehavior within the physical area of Age Work include many forms of brain injury (like cerebral palsy and lead poisoning), degenerative nervous system diseases (like Rett disorder), seizure disorders and developmental delay.

Within the social area of Age Work are found Autistic Spectrum Disorders and many forms of psychiatric illness.

Communication-related causes of hardwired misbehavior include such conditions as learning disabilities and many forms of deficient intelligence.

Disorders leading to hardwired misbehavior may be inherited from other generations or may be acquired through injury to brain or body. The effects of these disorders are not usually restricted to one skill area of Age Work. Indeed, it's most common to find two or all three areas of Age Work affected. For example, cerebral palsy and mental retardation usually impact all three skill areas of Age Work – physical, social and communication abilities.

Hardwired misbehavior always has two defining characteristics: It's associated with children's inability to consistently choose right behavior and children cannot willfully escape its underlying cause.

There are only two choices parents can make when hardwired misbehavior is identified: 1) They can change what's happening within the child and thus change the misbehavior, or 2) they can accept the underlying condition with its associated misbehavior and learn to live with it. Discipline is not an option for such misbehavior.

Some Examples of Hardwired Misbehavior

Misbehaviors like these can be treated and managed by therapists or doctors:

•Aborted suicide attempts due to depression – treated with psychotherapy and medication.

•Excessive soda drinking and weight loss due to diabetes – treated with insulin.

But these misbehaviors parents must learn to accept and live with:

•"Immaturity" due to mental retardation – treated with special curriculum in school and special accommodations in life.

•Inability to walk normally due to cerebral palsy – treated with physical and occupational therapy, braces, wheelchair.

Controlling Hardwired Misbehavior by changing internal processes

Some disorders, like diabetes or Bipolar Disorder, can be controlled or corrected with accurate diagnosis and treatment. Without accurate diagnosis, the symptoms of hardwired misbehavior might be mistaken for willful defiance. For example, weight loss from diabetes might be attributed to diet mania. Assaults on family members, a result of underlying Bipolar Disorder, might be interpreted as willful rebellion against authority.

Depression and Bipolar Disorder, lead poisoning and thyroid deficiency and many other physical and mental disorders are among the potential hidden causes of children's misbehavior. Identifying such underlying conditions and managing them allows Age Work to progress and restores choice-making ability. As you've seen, eliminating threats to Age Work reduces the intensity of severe misbehavior to either a moderate level, which may be effectively disciplined, or to a merely annoying level, which may be ignored.

Accepting Hardwired Misbehavior and learning to live with it

When hardwired misbehavior is truly caused by limitations in physical, social or communication skills, it's difficult or impossible to change. Effective discipline depends on children being free to make behavioral choices. Hardwired misbehavior, because it's not under children's control, doesn't permit choice-making. Internal events, which children can't control, force parents to accept and live with the resulting misbehavior.

Whenever we identify misbehavior due to abnormal Age Work we need to know:

●Can we change what's happening inside the child to improve or protect functioning within the skill areas of Age Work, or

●Must we accept and learn to live with the misbehavior?

Before we learn how to choose the best professional(s) to diagnose and treat hardwired misbehavior, let's learn an easy way to identify it. Recognizing hardwired misbehavior is a parent's job. No professional assistance is needed and no specific diagnosis is required. Indeed, as you'll soon see, parents who live with their children are often better equipped to suspect hardwired misbehavior than are professionals who see the children only briefly.

How to Recognize Hardwired Misbehavior

In recognizing hardwired misbehavior, understand children have *no choice* in acting it out. Limited ability and internal processes like physical or mental illness leave *no control* over such misbehavior. Limited ability and physical and mental illnesses all fall within the Consequence Area of Age Work. So, the first test for hardwired misbehavior is to see whether it affects Age Work.

Misbehavior occurring in the presence of normal performance in physical, social and communication areas cannot be hardwired (though we'll see what it is in a few pages). Misbehavior occurring in the presence of deficient performance in physical, social or communication areas *may* be hardwired and we'll need a second test to be sure. Remember, you can find the expected performance levels in the physical, social and communication areas for each age range simply presented in Appendix I.

The second and most reliable test for hardwired misbehavior is to check its "look" and "feel." Misbehavior of the hardwired type, done without choice or control, looks and feels very different from that done purposely and defiantly. You've already learned the emotional reactions created by moderate misbehavior are Confusion, Anxiety, or Anger. To pin down hardwired misbehavior most reliably, combine the "feel" of these emotional reactions with the "look" of the behavior as it's observed. Here's how it's done:

(We'll learn about Anger as a reaction to misbehavior and what causes it a bit later in this chapter.)

Many hidden causes of hardwiring are possible and some are listed, but you don't need to know any of them to recognize it. Simply use Appendix I to identify any delays in Age Work. Such delays, if present, are reliable indicators of hardwired misbehavior. Here follow some examples of the look and feel of hardwired misbehavior.

In an elementary schooler:

Elementary schoolers can hold pencils to write. They attend to their bathroom needs and talk to their teachers. An elementary schooler who can't hold a pencil, wets or soils clothing or doesn't speak intelligibly demonstrates delays in Age Work.

Observed Misbehavior	*Age Work Affected Skill(s)*	*Possible Disorders*	*"Hardwiring" Its Look & Feel*
Can't hold a pencil	*physical*	Cerebral Palsy Myasthenia Gravis	Non-selective No benefit *Anxiety*
Wets and soils clothes	*physical social*	Spinal tumor Autism	Non-selective No benefit *Anxiety*
Speech unintelligible	*physical communication*	Cleft palate Mental retardation	Non-selective No benefit *Confusion*

In an adolescent:

Adolescents should be able to engage in physical education activities at school. They're expected to maintain friendships without the help of alcohol or drugs and to sustain passing grades. When a teenager's strength, energy level and coordination deteriorate, friendships dry up, leading to isolation, and grades suddenly fall, Age Work is threatened.

Alan M. Davick, M.D.

When misbehavior is caused by internal, often unrecognized conditions, it *always* affects Age Work – physical, social, communication, or all three areas. In all cases of hardwired misbehavior timing is unpredictable, targets are non-selective, observers can discern no benefit to the child and it's often threatening to the child or others. Observing such behavior creates emotional reactions of Confusion or Anxiety, but almost never Anger.

Observed Misbehavior	Age Work Affected	Possible Disorders	"Hardwiring" Its Look & Feel
Poor stamina or incoordination	physical	Drug abuse Muscular Dystrophy	Non-selective Threatening Anxiety
Losing friends	social	Tourette Disorder Depression	No benefit Anxiety
Failing grades	communication	ADHD Alcoholism/Drug Use	No benefit Threatening Confusion

Before we can discipline moderate misbehavior, we must discover if children's choice-making has been blocked by hardwiring. That is, we must find out if underlying conditions are masking right choice-making or whether physical or mental limitations (like epilepsy, mental retardation, or Autism) will force us to accommodate to the misbehavior.

Now that you can recognize hardwired misbehavior, let's see how hidden causes can be uncovered and treated.

Hardwired Misbehavior: How to choose & use professionals

No matter how expert we are, even if we're child specialists, neither you nor I will ever be able to recognize all the hidden causes of misbehavior without help. That's because some mimic others and require special tests or techniques to be diagnosed. For example, lead and other heavy metal poisoning can be mistaken for mental retardation or a learning disability. Thyroid deficiency, depression, and many other physical and mental conditions can do likewise.

Once we've limited a child's misbehavior to the moderate level by STOPPING life-endangering misbehavior and ignoring the merely annoying, and before we can consider imposing discipline, we must ask ourselves if we suspect hardwired causes for the misbehavior. We must be sure the child can choose right alternatives. Recognizing and managing underlying causes of misbehavior is the only way we can assure ourselves a child has the *capability* to respond to discipline. To identify underlying disorders affecting behavior, we'll need professional assistance.

Over the years, I've narrowed the field of professionals who diagnose and treat hardwired behavior into three major categories: Physicians, psychologists, and educators.

There's an easy way to choose the right kind of professional(s) to diagnose and treat hardwiring. You need only take note of which skill areas of Age Work are affected by the misbehavior and consult professionals in this sequence:

- When *physical* skills are lagging, choose a physician.

- When *social* skills are deficient, choose a psychologist.

- When *communication* skills are inadequate, choose an educator.

When two or more areas of Age Work are affected by hardwired misbehavior choose professionals in this order: (See next page)

If several professionals are needed because several areas of Age Work are threatened, choosing professionals in this order will give you the best chance for proper diagnosis and treatment. That's because physical problems must be managed before social skills can be assessed and improved and because both physical and social skills must be restored before communication problems (including school-related achievement) can be remediated.

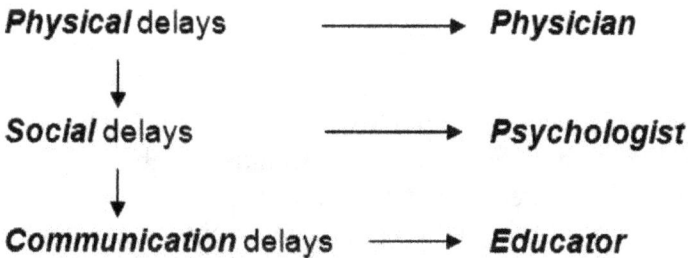

Physical delays   ⟶   **Physician**

        ↓

Social delays   ⟶   **Psychologist**

        ↓

Communication delays   ⟶   **Educator**

Once you suspect hardwired misbehavior, take note of which skill areas of Age Work are affected and decide upon the categories of professionals you'll need to consult for diagnosis and treatment. At this point you'll want to consider the qualifications of those professionals.

Though there are more names for specialists working with hardwired misbehavior than there are pages in this book, they all fall into one or another of the categories of physicians, psychologists, or educators. Each group, like cats, dogs, and children, have certain distinguishing differences, making it easy to tell one "species" from another. And like cats, dogs, and children, different experts within each category have learned to solve certain kinds of hardwiring problems better than others. In the following pages, the capabilities of each profession and some of the peculiarities of its members are presented.

Physicians and Hardwired Misbehavior

Physicians are medical doctors who are licensed to treat people with prescription medicines, hospitalization, and/or surgery. Pediatricians are physicians who treat children - often through eighteen years of age. They may further specialize and treat mental or nervous system disorders (developmental pediatricians), behavioral or learning problems (behavioral pediatricians), brain and nervous system conditions (pediatric neurologists), or severe emotional disturbances (child psychiatrists).

All physicians use similar steps to help solve a problem. First, they take a history. This means they ask lots of questions about how children got to be the way they are. Always included are questions about physical growth and development as well as possible diseases which may have contributed to the problem. Next, they perform a physical examination. Child psychiatrists, to avoid frightening a child, will often ask a pediatrician or other physician to do the physical examination to be sure no disease is present. Last, a treatment is recommended, often in the form of a prescription.

Physicians are trained to look for causes. When parents suspect physical problems are causing delays in Age Work, physicians can help them find out why. As you've seen, finding causes is essential to decide if underlying conditions can be changed by treatment, thus enabling discipline, or if one must accept the misbehavior and live with it.

• General and family practitioners, internists, and pediatricians are all "generalists" who can sort out problems. Any one of them may know parents and their families well enough to recognize hardwired misbehavior, but may not have specialized training to solve specific problems. In such cases, these physicians may refer parents to other physician-specialists who can solve those problems.

• Developmental/behavioral pediatricians have studied normal brain development in children. They've learned psychiatric and psychological techniques to identify hardwiring problems, especially physically-based misbehavior. Though they are trained to assess the social and communication components of Age Work as well, they do not usually treat these problems independently. For psychotherapy or the servicing of educational disorders, these physicians usually refer to psychologists or educators.

• Child neurologists specialize in physical disorders of the brain and nervous system. When hardwiring is suspected to be caused by physical conditions which seem to be getting worse, or in which ongoing damage to the nervous system may be occurring, child neurologists can perform tests to diagnose and organize treatment options. These physicians are not "generalists" and parents should not ask them to sort out causes for misbehavior.

• Child psychiatrists have training in child neurology, but do not usually do physical examinations. It is to child psychiatrists misbehaving children are referred after physical disease has been ruled out. Often, other professionals will have diagnosed problems in the social component of Age Work (e.g. explosive anger episodes, social isolation) requiring either a medicine or a search for a non-physical cause of the misbehavior. Child psychiatrists can be very costly, but while they are providing therapy, they, like other physicians, are able to prescribe medicines or hospitalize children. Like child neurologists, child psychiatrists are not "generalists" and parents should not ask them to sort out misbehavior problems.

Psychologists and Hardwired Misbehavior

Psychologists can be described as those who study the workings of the mind - especially feelings, desires and mental processes. By this definition, there are many more kinds of psychologists than there are types of physicians. If parents limit themselves to those psychologists who study and treat humans, especially children, it will be easier to understand this group of specialists. Even so, parents need to know some psychologists are called "social workers" while some professionals called "school psychologists" are educators (we'll learn about them below).

Psychologists who diagnose and treat children are certified or licensed to do so. They are not medical doctors, though they may have either a Ph.D. (Doctor of Philosophy in Psychology), a Psy.D. (Doctor of Psychology), an M.A. or M.S. (Master of Arts or Science), or other advanced degree. They do not perform physical examinations on children, but rather assess problems by using tests of intelligence, achievement, educational skills or emotional functioning. All members of this group give therapy, but the range of services differs for each one.

In the following paragraphs I'll describe some of the important differences between groups of psychologists, which will help you decide which to use. Some psychologists do not follow the general statements made here. I strongly suggest checking with any psychologist you plan to use before committing to that individual. You need to be certain the services you need will be provided. For example, if people at different stages of life in your family are having difficulty with their relationships to one another, choose a psychologist who specializes in family therapy.

- Clinical child psychologists are experts who assess and give therapy for misbehavior affecting the *social* component of Age Work. Though they also diagnose misbehavior affecting *communication* skills, after diagnosis such problems are referred for service to educators, a third group of professionals discussed below. There are two subcategories within the group of clinical child psychologists; analytic and behavioral psychologists:

• Analytic child psychologists follow the psychiatric tradition and spend considerable time searching for causes of misbehavior. Sometimes years are spent in analysis, looking for causes for what a child says and does. The goal is to help develop insight or understanding, and so help the child control or change the misbehavior.

• Behavioral child psychologists focus on the actual behavior. After collecting information about the misbehavior, a plan or strategy is designed to change it. This is more direct than the analytic approach, and I recommend it because it's faster and less costly. If it fails to work after a reasonable period of time, a parent can always reconsider the analytic approach.

• Psychiatric social workers are a special group of social workers who diagnose and give therapy for misbehavior affecting the social component of Age Work. They can also assess misbehavior affecting the communication component of Age Work, but refer such problems to educators for remediation. Psychiatric social workers usually have a master's degree, though some have a doctorate. Social workers' additional knowledge about society's systems and agencies may be of particular benefit in cases, for example, of juvenile delinquency, drug, sex, or physical abuse.

When you identify misbehavior affecting the social skill area of Age Work causing Anxiety or Confusion, a psychologist is the best type of professional to start with. If the psychologist suspects hardwiring affecting the physical or communication skill areas of Age Work, referral will be made to a physician or an educator, respectively.

Let's look at the third category of professionals, the educators. Within this group are school psychologists. School psychologists working exclusively within schools and not providing therapy I classify as educators rather than psychologists.

Educators and Hardwired Misbehavior

A common element in the category of educators is their focus on the performance of children in schools, whether day by day classroom instruction, achievement testing and improvement of academic performance, or administration of the school and its staff. These professionals do not perform physical examinations, write medical prescriptions or give psychotherapy. Though educators assess school-related problems using a variety of tests, they rarely search for basic causes. Their evaluations help to define misbehavior and label it. This information is then used to develop an Individual Educational Program, or IEP, to assist children's educational progress.

Educators comprise the most diverse of the categories of professionals. They include:

•Principals (and vice principals)

•Teachers

•School counselors; Pupil personnel workers

•School psychologists (educational psychologists, psychometrists)

•Educational specialists (math, speech and language, reading)

•Occupational and physical therapists (perceptual-motor specialists)

•Audiologists

•School Nurses

When you identify hardwiring affecting only the communication skill area of Age Work and causing Anxiety or Confusion, an educator is the best professional to begin with. If the educator suspects hardwiring due to a physical or social component of Age Work, parents you'll be advised to consult a physician or a psychologist.

One last word about hardwired misbehavior and professionals. Sometimes, you won't know how to convert severe misbehavior to a moderate level without professional help.

Whenever you encounter severe misbehavior you need to STOP, but where violence or physical self-injury are not immediate issues (for which a 911 call is most appropriate), look at the affected skill areas and choose a professional helper in this order:

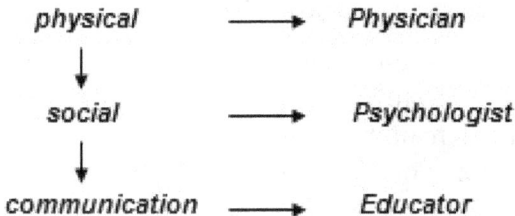

physical   ⟶   Physician

↓

social   ⟶   Psychologist

↓

communication   ⟶   Educator

This is a good place for you to stop a moment and take a bow! You began learning how to discipline your child without going to jail by recognizing misbehavior and assigning it to severe, moderate, or merely annoying categories. You STOPPED severe misbehavior with whatever legal means were required and you chose to ignore merely annoying misbehavior. Having thus eliminated life-endangering misbehavior and the merely annoying, you limited your focus to moderate misbehavior and considered possible underlying, hardwired causes requiring professional help to diagnose and treat. You learned to suspect hardwired misbehavior when you experienced feelings of *Confusion* or *Anxiety* observing it.

Let's turn now to misbehavior that generates Anger as you watch it.

The significance of anger as a response to misbehavior

Oppositional-Defiant Misbehavior–its look & feel

What It Looks Like (Your observation)	*What It Feels Like* (Your emotional reaction)
The misbehavior is manipulative	*annoyance*
• It's *predictable*. • It's *selective*, targeting some people, not others.	
....and/or...	
• It *challenges Authority*, forcing someone to do or allow something unacceptable.	*Anger*

Okay, you've cooled life-endangering misbehavior to a moderate, manageable level and are ignoring merely annoying misbehavior. As you observe the remaining misbehavior, rather than experiencing Anxiety or Confusion, you experience Anger.

Anger-generating misbehavior, unlike hardwired misbehavior, is caused by children's willful defiance. That is to say, children engage in such behavior *by choice*. Because they choose to engage in the misbehavior, children decide when it occurs, to whom it's directed, in what location it will occur and what they hope to achieve by it. Anger is created in an observer who is either forced to accept undesirable consequences or to perform unpleasant acts as a result of the misbehavior.

Unlike misbehavior caused by underlying mental or physical conditions beyond a child's control, oppositional and defiant misbehavior need not affect Age Work, but it *always* disturbs or threatens Others and Authority. Just as hardwired misbehavior is recognized by its "look" and "feel," oppositional and defiant misbehavior can be recognized by its own look and feel.

When oppositional-defiant misbehavior challenges Authority and seems to indicate children are doing whatever they want, you can be sure their actions were chosen for a reason and the reason is always the same. Children choose to be defiant because they anticipate desirable (from their perspective, naturally) consequences. This is the essence of defiant misbehavior. The environment within which children devise actions to achieve (what they consider) desirable consequences, is accessible only at certain times and at certain places. The former attribute makes defiant behavior *predictable*, while the latter makes it *selective*. The challenge to Authority defines the behavior as misbehavior and provokes feelings of annoyance or Anger in the observer. As previously mentioned, oppositional-defiant misbehavior need not affect Age Work or Others, though it always affects Authority.

Though children engage in defiant misbehavior to achieve their own ends, parents don't need to know what's motivating them in order to recognize the misbehavior as defiant. Here are some examples of defiant misbehavior. Note it can occur at any age.

<u>In an infant</u>:

Grandparents report an eight-month-old infant arches its back, shrieks and never coos at them when it's held on their laps. Later, with the parents, the baby sits quietly and coos. Scoring observed threats to the physical, social and communication areas of Age Work and their emotional reactions to the baby's behavior, as you've learned to do earlier, the grandparents see a threat to their Authority (1 degree), a threat to the *social* skill area of Age Work (1 degree), an ill effect on their relationship to the baby as a pair of Others (1 degree) and feel *annoyed* (1 degree). They have recorded a score of 4 degrees, qualifying as a moderate form of misbehavior. This misbehavior must be defiant and not hardwired because it's predictable, targets only some people and challenges their Authority. And, the grandparents feel no *Confusion* or *Anxiety*.

Observed Misbehavior	Consequence Areas Affected	Possible Causes	Defiance Its "Look" & "Feel"
Baby shrieks	Authority - 1°	Wants parents	Selective
Won't coo	Others - 1°	Fright	Predictable
	Age Work		
	- *social* - 1°		*annoyance* - 1°
	Total: <u>4°</u>		

Occasionally, observing a child's misbehavior generates both Anger *and* Confusion or Anxiety; that is, the misbehavior qualifies as *both* hardwired and oppositional-defiant. Don't panic! Trust your feelings! Both types of misbehavior are present and you'll need professional help to diagnose and treat underlying disorders *before* you do anything about the defiance. To get the most effective professional help for "mixed" misbehavior, note the skill areas of Age Work affected and choose professionals in the previously suggested sequence:

•When physical skills are lagging, choose a physician.

•When social skills are deficient, choose a psychologist.

•When communication skills are inadequate, choose an educator.

When two or more areas of Age Work are affected, by hardwired misbehavior, choose professionals in this order:

Physician > Psychologist > Educator

Here are two examples of oppositional-defiance. In the first example, mere *annoyance* is generated and no "hardwiring" is suspected. In the second example, oppositional-defiant misbehavior is superimposed on an underlying condition, creating "mixed" reactions of *annoyance* and *Anxiety*. In scoring "mixed" reactions, the higher point emotional reaction is chosen:

In an elementary schooler:

A math teacher reports an elementary schooler keeps calling out and dropping his pencil in class. Lessons are disrupted when classmates laugh and become unruly. Neither his parents nor other teachers see this occur elsewhere. Since the math teacher's Authority (1 degree) is threatened, Others, including classmates and teacher (2 degrees) are disturbed and the math teacher is *annoyed* (1 degree), moderate misbehavior is defined with a score of 4 degrees.

Observed Misbehavior	*Consequence Areas affected*	*Possible Causes*	*Defiance Its "Look" & "Feel"*
Calls out Drops pencil in math class	Authority - 1° Others - 2°	Unprepared Disrespects teacher	Selective Predictable *annoyance* - 1

Total: <u>4</u>°

Because the misbehavior is predictable and selective (occurring only in math class), challenges Authority and provokes *annoyance*, it must be defiant misbehavior.

Now imagine the same scenario with one difference; though the child continues to call out only in math class, all the teachers and the parents notice the child's fingers getting weaker over several weeks until he can no longer hold a pencil. Even feeding himself with utensils becomes difficult. The effects of this misbehavior may still *annoy* the teacher(s), but *Confusion* or *Anxiety* will likely also be provoked, certainly in the parents. Dropping pencils everywhere with progressive weakness of fingers is *non-selective, of no benefit, Anxiety*-provoking or *Confusing* and affects the *physical* skill area of Age Work. This qualifies as hardwired misbehavior and requires diagnosis and treatment by a physician before the defiant component, characterized by calling out only in math class, can be addressed.

Observed Misbehavior	Consequence Areas affected	Possible Causes	Defiance Its "Look" & "Feel"
Calls out only in math class	Authority - 1° Others - 2°	Unprepared Disrespectful	Selective Predictable annoyance*
Drops pencils, trouble eating everywhere	Age Work -physical - 1°	Brain/muscle disease	Non-selective Anxiety - 2°
		Total: 6°	

* Note only the more intense emotion (Anxiety) is scored.

Calling out only in math class, still predictable, selective and annoying, remains defiant misbehavior, but cannot be disciplined until underlying conditions are diagnosed and treated.

How to Simplify "Mixed" Misbehavior

Complex misbehavior, representing all the "bad stuff" children do, is really nothing more than a mixture of hardwired and oppositional-defiant misbehavior. It may remain merely annoying or it may intensify to moderate or severe levels.

Once you've decided to ignore merely annoying misbehavior and have STOPPED severe misbehavior with whatever degree of (legal) force is required (including a 911 call or psychiatric hospital admission), you'll have isolated moderate misbehavior. Moderate misbehavior allows you time to discover and manage causes with professional help. Then, when hardwired components have been identified and managed, any residual annoying misbehavior may be ignored and attention directed to moderate, willful, oppositional-defiance. This form of misbehavior will be the target of our disciplinary efforts and is the subject of the remaining chapters of this book.

The Professional Idiocy: *Only professionals are qualified to decide if, how and when children should be disciplined.**

*Adapted from Managing Misbehavior in Kids: The *MIS*/Kidding® Process
Alan M. Davick, M.D., MIS/KIDDING, LLC, 2014

64

Chapter Four

Disciplinary models for oppositional-defiant misbehavior

We've seen how defiant misbehavior provokes *annoyance* or *Anger* in the observer by assaulting Authority. We've learned children always have a reason for defiant behavior and the reason is always the same; they anticipate an inappropriate reward for their misbehavior (like watching their parents lose their cool!). Indeed, when children chose to do something they shouldn't do or refuse to do something they should do, they look forward to an inappropriate reward they consider more seductive or compelling than any other rewards they're aware of. As we'll soon see, the secret to effective discipline is to present defiant children with more powerful, but appropriate rewards for right behavior than those they anticipate for misbehavior.

Let's examine two forms of defiance a bit more closely; *actively* doing what you're not supposed to do and *passively* choosing not to do what you're supposed to do.

The Energy Content of Active & Passive Defiance

Active Defiance

Choosing to do things you're not supposed to do is an active form of misbehavior demanding energy from children. The greater the intensity of the misbehavior, the greater the amount of energy required. In devising strategies to discipline defiant behavior, we'll do best if we utilize that energy to promote right behavior rather than trying to snuff it out and thereby waste it.

Of course, if you're a babysitter or other part-time caretaker in authority and have only limited time to react to defiant behavior, snuffing it out it may be all you have time to do. For full-time authority persons, like parents or grandparents, harnessing the energy of active defiance provides an opportunity to move children furthest along the path to responsible adulthood.

Here are some examples of active defiance:

- A ten-month-old baby crying whenever its parents lay it down

- A three-year-old hitting its playmates, unprovoked

- A ten-year-old using foul language in school

- A sixteen-year-old stealing money from parents

Passive Defiance

When children refuse to do things they're supposed to do, they're engaging in passive defiance. The energy children devote to passive defiance is much less than that for active defiance, so there's less energy to harness for discipline. As a result, this form of misbehavior requires us to create motivation for children to pursue right behavior.

Here are some examples of passive defiance:

- A ten-month-old refusing to hold its own bottle

- A three-year-old communicating only by gesture to a certain teacher

- A ten-year-old failing to turn off the TV when finished watching

- A fifteen-year-old consistently leaving dirty clothes on the bedroom floor

Remember, whenever children fail to do what they're supposed to do, we need to test for hardwiring. In other words, we need to be sure a child is defiant (that is, refusing to perform) rather than being unable to choose right behavior (as with underlying physical or mental disorders).

As we've seen, clues to willful defiance are the Anger it provokes and the fact it targets certain people in certain places. By contrast, misbehavior stemming from physical or mental disorders, and not under a child's control, creates Confusion or Anxiety in the observer, is non-selective of its targets, occurs randomly (anywhere, anytime) and is often harmful to the child.

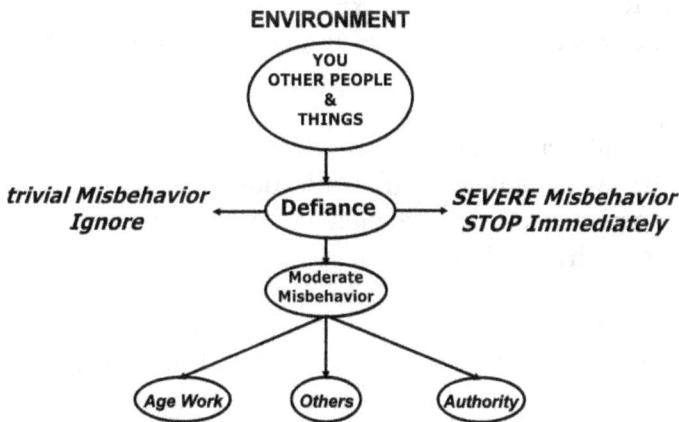

ENVIRONMENT

```
              YOU
         OTHER PEOPLE
              &
           THINGS

trivial Misbehavior  ←  Defiance  →  SEVERE Misbehavior
     Ignore                            STOP Immediately

              Moderate
             Misbehavior

      Age Work      Others      Authority
```

If underlying physical or mental conditions are suspected, we'll need to diagnose causes with professional help and determine if we can change the behavior or if we need to accept it and live with it.

Now let's see how inappropriate rewards lure children toward defiance and how we can replace them with alternative and more powerful rewards to discipline children.

The environmental bubble at the top of the adjacent diagram includes You, Other People and Things. These parts of children's surroundings may offer temptations to children to engage in defiance. Though children experience their environment through all five senses of hearing, vision, taste, touch and smell, by far the two most influential are what is seen and what is heard. Children are always watching and listening how you, other people and things react to their behavior. Since you may not have control over what other people and things communicate to children, you as an Authority person must be prepared to overwhelm inappropriate rewards from any source with more powerful inducements for right behavior.

Communication from the environment: words vs. actions

Environmental experiences are created by what parents say and do as well as by the communication and actions of other people and things in the vicinity of children. What the environment "says" and "does" are forms of language. We may call what is said, word language and what occurs or what is done as a result of behavior, action language.

If we tell children what they're doing is good or bad, we communicate word language. If, while doing what they're doing, children experience something pleasant or unpleasant (see, hear, feel, taste or smell), that's action language.

If we act differently from the way we say we do; that is, if our action language is different from our word language, children believe what they see, feel, taste or smell rather than what they hear. This is because they've learned what we say is often inconsistent while what is seen, felt, tasted or smelled is more often consistent and predictable.

Within their environment (of which parents are a part), children are constantly checking word language against action language. When word language is inconsistent with action language, children consider the word language "dishonest" and act in accordance with more "honest" action language.

Let's see how we can use this principle to develop and energize powerful disciplinary models to manage active and passive defiance. We'll present the models to children with word language and energize them with action language.

Word language commands & action language consequences – the disciplinary models

Word language (what we say) expresses our wishes. Even when wishes are voiced as commands, they're only wishes and have no power of their own. Discipline in the form of word language is like the wiring of a motor; someone's physical design to guide energy through a device to achieve a goal. But until discipline is energized, it's merely a wish to discipline and cannot achieve its goal. In order to energize discipline, it must be connected to an action language consequence.

Action language is like formless energy, crackling and popping in all directions, sometimes pleasant, sometimes hurtful. When discipline is presented to a child in the form of word language (a verbal request) and linked to action language (a predicted consequence to be experienced by the child) a *Discipline Command* is created. Disciplinary commands are extremely powerful and effective.

The components of each of the discipline models that follow will always be the same; a word language request linked to action language consequences – either rewards, punishments or both. The forms of discipline used for active defiance are designed differently from those used for passive defiance. Those used by (full-time) parents are different from those used by part-time authority persons, like babysitters.

In the remainder of this chapter we'll learn how to choose models of discipline for different forms of defiance and for the varying roles assumed by different caretakers. In the next chapter, we'll see how these models are activated with powerful action language consequences to create disciplinary commands.

Energizing discipline for active defiance

There are three disciplinary commands designed to control active defiance. For children who choose to do things they're not supposed to do, we may use the Brick Wall model, the Billiard model or the Distraction model to control their defiance. The design of each of these forms of discipline is a bit different and each requires a bit different strategy by the authority person. Depending upon the time and energy you have in your authority role, you may find one or another form of discipline most suitable.

To better understand the strengths and weaknesses of the Brick Wall, the Billiard and the Distraction models of discipline, let's begin by diagramming what defiant children are really up to. Oppositional and defiant behavior always follows the same path; children have decided to pursue an inappropriate goal they anticipate is more rewarding than right behavior:

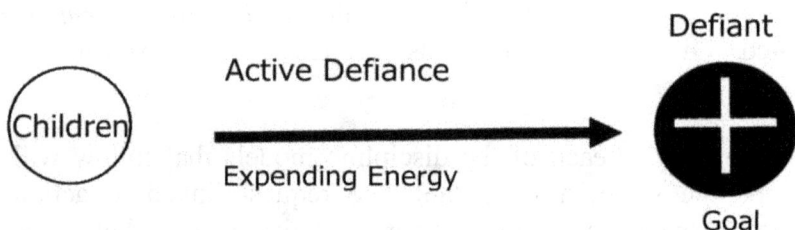

In active defiance, children expend energy trying to reach an inappropriate goal. Rather than being indifferent or lackadaisical, the children are actually motivated, often highly motivated, to achieve the inappropriate goal. Let's examine three forms of discipline used to manage active defiance.

Discipline in the Brick Wall Mode

Blocking willful defiance with a punishment at least as powerful as a child's inappropriate goal is the quickest, but most energy-wasting, form of discipline. Standing directly in the path of such active defiance, like a brick wall, requires you to expend at least as much energy as the child does and you'll need to absorb the splash-back of depression or anger it generates in the child.

Discipline in the Brick Wall mode translates as, "Stop it, (or else!)," where the "or else" is a punishment. Discipline in this mode is most attractive to part-time caretakers and to parents rushed for time because it's the fastest acting form of discipline. The power and effectiveness of Brick Wall discipline in stopping defiance comes from the fact there are almost no limits (except jail!) to the intensity of punishment. And as you'll see in the next chapter, this form of discipline is the easiest type to verbalize and energize, requiring very little planning and working equally well for children of all ages.

Here's what discipline in the Brick Wall mode looks like:

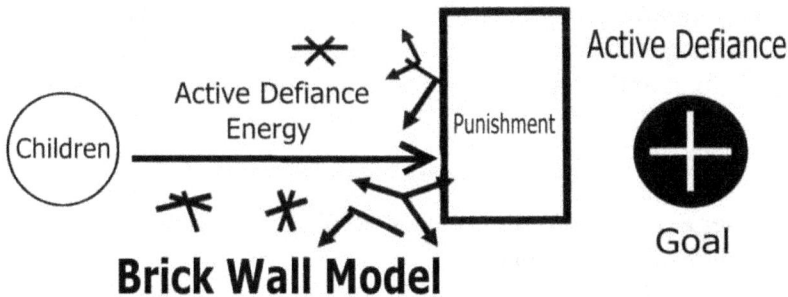

Brick Wall Model

Note how a wall of punishment blocks children's access to a defiant goal, but the children's misdirected energy splatters off the wall. Blocking oppositional behavior with a punishment squanders children's motivation which might otherwise be redirected toward right behavior. It also creates depression or anger, the latter of which usually ricochets in the face of authority! Disciplinary commands in the Brick Wall mode, though they're easiest to employ, are the least efficient and most dangerous form of discipline.

Don't worry about punishments and rewards now. I'll show you how to choose them and use them in the next chapter. Let's look at some examples of discipline in the Brick Wall mode, used to stop active defiance.

Using Discipline in the Brick Wall Mode: "Stop it "or else!"

<u>For a ten-month-old baby</u>

Here's an example of Brick Wall discipline for a ten-month-old baby who cries whenever its parents put it down. It's not important for the baby to understand the word language since the action language speaks for itself:

"Stop crying, or (we'll leave the room)."

The first time this command is given, most babies will cry longer and harder. The command, including its linked punishment, must be repeated several times before the baby tests the command for its consistency and discovers crying doesn't achieve its inappropriate goal (of having the parents stay with it indefinitely.) Once the command is discovered to be honest and consistent, the baby will remain quiet to gain the parents' presence.

<u>For a three-year-old</u>

Here's another example of Brick Wall discipline for a three-year-old hitting its playmates unprovoked:

"Stop hitting or (you'll go to the time out room.)"

As in the first example, this child will likely test the command and end up screaming or crying in the time out room. This child's motivation for hitting the playmates hasn't been vented, redirected, or even identified. It's been "splattered" against the punishment of going to time out.

<u>For a ten-year-old</u>

Brick Wall discipline for a ten-year-old using foul language in school might be presented like this:

"If any teachers complain you curse in school, (you'll be grounded for a week.)"

Since the only way you'd know about continued defiance by this ten-year old would be complaints from teachers, the discipline is aimed at stopping complaints.

<u>For a sixteen-year-old</u>

Here's Brick Wall discipline for a sixteen-year-old who takes his parents' belongings without permission:

"If you take things without permission, (you won't be allowed to drive.)"

This form of discipline, because it splatters children's misdirected energy against a brick wall of punishment, bounces back in face of the authority as either anger or depression. These reactions intensify misbehavior. Sometimes, anger or depression reach life-endangering levels, either for the child or for others. For example, the three-year-old in time out might resort to wetting, soiling, or even self-mutilation. The grounded ten-year-old might begin physically attacking siblings and the teenager might ignore curfews or even steal a car.

In general, the more effort and energy children devote to defiance, the greater the risk of bounce-back. There are two better forms of discipline for controlling active defiance. They utilize children's misdirected energies to achieve right behavior with less or even no splatter. The first of these, discipline in the Billiard mode is diagrammed below:

Using Discipline in the Billiard Mode

In the Billiard mode of discipline, punishment is used to deflect a child away from misbehavior while, at the same time, a reward is offered to pull the child toward right behavior. Though some anger or depression occur if the child chooses to test the command, the

Billiard model preserves most of a child's motivational energy to pursue appropriate goals.

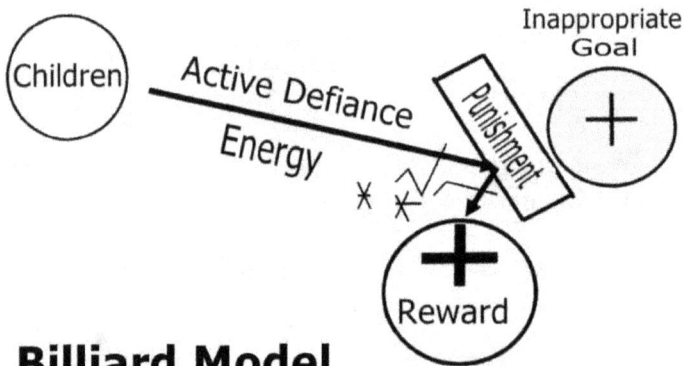

Billiard Model

Like the Brick Wall discipline, the Billiard model works rapidly to stop defiance, but takes more planning to construct because, in contrast to punishments, which are similar for most children and which are effective over most age ranges, compelling rewards are different for different children. For now, let's focus only on the structure of the various forms of discipline. We'll learn all about powerful and compelling rewards in the next chapter.

Here are some examples of discipline in the Billiard mode:

Examples of Discipline in the Billiard Mode

Word language commands in the Billiard mode are phrased, "Stop that or (punishment); do this instead and (reward)." In the following examples, phrases in parentheses are either a punishment or a reward:

For a ten-month-old baby

Here's Billiard discipline for a ten-month-old baby crying whenever its parents put it down. As before, the baby need not understand the words. Action language speaks for itself:

"When you cry, (we'll put you down); when you're quiet (we'll pick you up)."

In this situation, the baby will cry several times when it's put down, but it will discover that its parents can be lured back with silence. Eventually, much of the energy the baby directed at crying (active defiance) will be redirected at quiet play with the parents (right behavior).

For a three-year-old

For the three-year-old who hits his playmates unprovoked, discipline in the Billiard mode might look like this:

"Stop hitting or (you'll go to the time-out room); if you help Johnny fill his pail with sand (you may have an ice cream)."

For a ten-year-old

For the ten-year-old using foul language in school:

"If your teachers complain about your language, (you'll be grounded); if your teachers tell me you've been courteous this week (we'll go fishing)."

For a sixteen-year-old

For the teenager taking parents' belongings without permission:

"If you take things without asking, (you'll be forbidden to drive for a month); if you consistently ask permission when you use our things, (your curfew will be extended to midnight.)"

Billiard discipline is safer than Brick Wall discipline for children engaging in active defiance because it creates less anger or depression. Punishments can be chosen without intimate knowledge of children's likes and dislikes. The punishments within these commands deflect ongoing defiance even if the rewards are poorly chosen. When rewards are well chosen they preserve children's motivation to pursue right behavior. I recommend the Billiard form of discipline as the model of choice when time is of the essence and your energies as an authority are limited.

A third form of discipline can be used for controlling defiance. Distraction, diagrammed below, is best reserved for less intense levels of moderate active defiance and for passive defiance. Discipline in Distraction mode uses two or more rewards presented together to distract the child away from misbehavior.

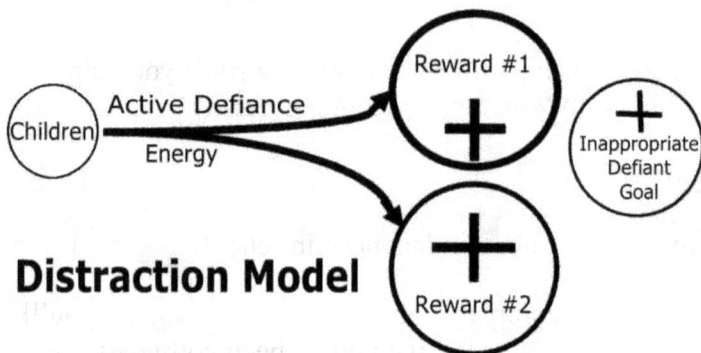

When children are not highly motivated or intent on their misbehavior, Distraction offers a way to move them away from misbehavior without creating any anger or depression.

Discipline in the Distraction Mode

Distraction takes longer to work than either Brick Wall or Billiard forms of discipline. Since no punishment is used, children continue their misguided efforts until they discover rewards for compliance are more desirable than misbehavior. The weakness of Distraction is if the chosen rewards are not compelling enough, defiance continues. Distraction takes patience and requires intimate knowledge of children in order to find rewards powerful enough to be effective. That's why it works best for parents.

Here are some disciplinary commands in Distraction mode:

Examples of Discipline in the Distraction Mode

Discipline in the Distraction mode is phrased, "Do this instead and you may have (reward #1); or do that instead and you may have (reward #2)." In the following examples, rewards are placed in parentheses.

For a ten-month-old baby

"Sit quietly on the bed and (we'll give you your bottle) or sit quietly in the bathtub and (you can play with your floating toys)."

This command works only if the parents know the baby wants its bottle or likes the tub. For some babies, either reward may be unattractive or even interpreted as punishment. Under the best of circumstances, it will take time for the baby to discover and switch goals.

For the three-year-old hitting playmates

"Help Johnny fill his pail with sand and (you may have ice cream) or tell Johnny you're sorry and (we'll go on the merry-go-round)."

For the ten-year-old using foul language in school

"Go to school two weeks with no complaints about your language and (we'll go fishing); or bring a letter home from your teacher complimenting you on being respectful and (we'll go to Disney World)."

For the teenager taking things without permission

"Ask our permission before using our things for the next month and (your curfew will be extended to midnight) or, if you prefer, (your allowance will be increased)."

Discipline in the Distraction mode is useful for either active or passive defiance, though it takes more thought to construct and more time to work. Its advantage over forms of discipline using punishment is it doesn't provoke anger or depression. Children's full energies are diverted to right behavior. The diagram and examples shown above use two rewards, but you can use as many rewards as you wish, depending upon your knowledge of your child.

When children are being passively defiant, they are refusing to do things they're supposed to do. And by doing nothing, they are experiencing what they consider a rewarding outcome. They see no reason to pursue right behavior. In this situation, we need to create motivation where none exists. This can be achieved by using discipline in Hansel & Gretel mode, designed to attract an unmotivated child toward right behavior.

Discipline in Hansel & Gretel Mode–Used for Passive Defiance

Think of passive defiance as a form of misbehavior in which children are content to sit on inappropriate goals rather than expending energy to defy authority. They aren't *actively* misbehaving. Rather, they're simply failing to pursue right behavior. As in the examples of Distraction mode, Hansel & Gretel discipline uses no punishment and doesn't risk provoking depression or anger. It leads children toward right behavior with a trail of rewards.

Here follows a diagram of discipline in the Hansel & Gretel mode. Notice how a series of rewards offered in sequence entice a child toward compliance:

78

Hansel & Gretel Model

Discipline in the Hansel & Gretel mode is most suitable for truly passive defiance. But, if defiance seems to require punishment to stop it, you're likely dealing with *active* misbehavior and another form of discipline will be better suited to manage it.

Using Discipline in the Hansel & Gretel Mode for Passive Defiance

Here are some disciplinary commands in the Hansel & Gretel mode designed to motivate children to move toward right behavior. Discipline in the Hansel & Gretel mode is phrased, "Do this and (reward #1); continue doing this and (bigger reward #2), etc." The trail of rewards in this mode may number one, two, or several. As in previous examples, rewards are enclosed by parentheses.

For a ten-month-old refusing to hold her own bottle

"Hold your bottle and (I'll carry you outside)."

For a three-year-old using only gesture to communicate to a teacher

"When you tell me what you want, (I'll let you have it)."

For a ten-year-old failing to turn off the TV when finished

"Turn off the TV when you're finished and (you may watch it tomorrow)."

<u>For a teenager leaving dirty clothes on the floor</u>

"Throw your dirty clothes in the hamper this week and (you may invite your friend to sleep over this weekend); throw your clothes in the hamper for four weeks and (we'll host a party here for your friends)."

Don't worry if you can't always tell passive from active defiance. It's a matter of opinion and yours is as good as the next person's! Besides, the distinction is made only as a guide to choosing among disciplinary models. If you make a mistake and use a more powerful word language command for defiance, it will still work, perhaps even faster.

Discipline in the Billiard, Distraction or Hansel & Gretel modes requires knowledge of children's likes and dislikes because they depend on rewards. This familiarity is needed to choose powerful enough rewards to overwhelm inappropriate goals. Neither Distraction nor Hansel & Gretel forms of discipline employs any punishment and both of these models depend upon the choice of effective rewards to succeed. For this reason alone, parents are more likely to use these forms of discipline than babysitters and part-time caretakers.

There are other, more important differences than available time and patience between parents and part-time caretakers. If you're a parent, identifying your disciplinary goals will help you choose the best word language commands to promote right behavior.

Choosing the Right Form of Discipline: What Are Parents For?

All authorities need to control defiance. But parents must do more than merely stop misbehavior. They must encourage right behavior.

We've seen how misbehavior is recognized by its destructive effects on Age Work and relationships to Others and Authority. Constructive effects on the Consequence Areas define right behavior.

What makes growth within the Consequence Areas so important? It's because children's success in life depends on achieving self-fulfillment (Age Work), getting along with other people (Others) and reasonable acceptance of rules (Authority). But, in my opinion, growth in the Consequence Areas is not itself the ultimate goal of parenting. I believe the ultimate goal for parents is to create responsible adults. Right behavior permits this process to occur, but it doesn't ensure it. To lead children to responsible adulthood, parents must furnish three "provisions" for adulthood. Together, they form what I call the HoNoR Role:

*H*onest word language commands

o

*N*urturance through love and affection

o

*R*esponsibility for consequences

The HoNoR Role of parenthood distinguishes parents from other caretakers. Whenever misbehavior occurs, opportunities present themselves for parents to equip children with more of these provisions for adulthood. Fortunately, the HoNoR Role requires less effort than most other approaches to parenthood and it's the most effective method of applying discipline.

The Importance of Honesty in Choosing Word Language Commands

Cats and dogs are rarely seen ducking their heads in bowls of water or walking on hot stoves. That's because water and hot stoves consistently "speak" in action language. Water always says, "If you keep your head in me you'll drown." Hot stoves always say, "If you walk on me I'll burn you." After one or two tests of this action language, it becomes clear to the animals that defying this language consistently results in choking or burning. Soon, the animals avoid immersing their heads in any body of water or coming in contact with any hot object. The consistency of this action language defines it as "honest". That is, there's never any confusion about the meaning of the action language.

As authority persons, but especially as parents, we want children to learn to trust us. They've got to know they can rely on how their parents portray the world. They need to figure out which rules they must follow, which they may follow and which they can ignore. Being honest with children is the single most important job parents have – more important even than showing them affection.

When parents act dishonestly by intentionally overlooking or even rewarding misbehavior, children will eventually be hurt or killed. Affection cannot save children from parental dishonesty. Indeed, dishonest messages from parents, others or things, are the source of children's defiance.

Some examples of parental dishonesty are worth reviewing:

A toddler tests for Honesty: Bobby's in the kitchen again!

Bobby, age two and a half years, watches Mommy frosting a cake. He reaches for the icing and Mommy says, "No! You mustn't!" Bobby pauses. But he's tasted icing before. Its action language says, "Eating icing tastes good." When faced with these conflicting messages - word language expressing a wish and action language recalling a rewarding experience - Bobby reaches for the cake again.

Mommy hasn't thought about conflicting messages from the environment, of which she's a part. If she continues to present word language wishes unattached to action language consequences her wishes will continue to be ignored. Once such a pattern is established, more important wishes will likely be ignored as well, leading to potentially serious misbehavior.

An elementary schooler tests for Honesty: Jefferson gets a shot

Five-year-old Jefferson is brought to the doctor's office for a shot. While he sits on Mommy's lap, she explains, "The shot won't hurt" (a dishonest comment). She tells him to sit still and not to move when the doctor gives the shot (a word language wish). When the doctor arrives with the needle, Mommy clutches Jefferson tightly, breathes deeply and tries to bury his head on her shoulder (action language translation: "This is terrible! It will hurt. I will try to protect you from the doctor. Even I'm scared!") Jefferson accepts the action language messages while ignoring the word language. He jumps off Mom's lap, writhes and screams and hides under a table. It takes the doctor, two assistants and Daddy to hold Jefferson for his shot while Mommy tearfully excuses herself.

Beside the dishonest word language that the shot wouldn't hurt, the whole event transmits many action language messages to Jefferson:

•The doctor is a monster who's trying to hurt you.

•Mommy acts like she'll protect you from monsters, but when she sees one, she abandons you.

•Mommy told a lie. The shot did hurt. Next time, better to bite the doctor first, before he kills you!

Jefferson's Mommy is suffering guilt over having to subject her son to a painful, but necessary shot. In an attempt to abort anticipated active defiance on Jefferson's part, Mommy offers the reward of affection (saying kind words, hugging) *before* Jefferson has had a chance to behave well. You may recall this is the essence of bribery. Worse, Mommy also offers dishonest word language – "The shot won't hurt." As you've learned, bribes and dishonest word language comprise a recipe for misbehavior. Jefferson's experience at the doctor's office almost guarantees worse behavior the next time.

Knowing what you now know, Mom might better have used a word language command to impose discipline in either the Billiard or Distraction mode. We'll see examples of discipline for Jefferson in the next chapter.

An adolescent tests for honesty: Debbie is starting to abuse alcohol

Debbie, seventeen-years-old, is growing up. She can't wait to be seen doing all the things grown-ups do. Some of her more grown-up friends are drinking alcohol. She tries it, too, although she doesn't really like it at first. Her Mom finds beer cans in her room. She forbids Debbie to drink alcohol (a word language wish), telling her it's dangerous (more word language).

Debbie sees her parents take a drink or two every day. She's heard alcohol is "supposed" to harm you, but Mom and Dad don't seem worried (action language: Drinking may hurt some people, but not us). Also, Debbie sees many grown-ups drinking without apparent ill effects (action language: If you're grown-up, you can drink – no one takes the possibility of disease very seriously). She continues to sneak beer into the house until her consumption of alcohol affects her stamina, her school grades, and even her friendships.

Eventually, her parents take her to the pediatrician who confirms Debbie is an alcoholic.

Debbie's parents, like those in the preceding examples, are unaware of the many conflicting action language messages received by their daughter. In spite of their true concerns for Debbie's health, they seem unable to impose effective discipline in the early stages of Debbie's defiance. They are now facing severe misbehavior which they must STOP with all available means.

They will need to lower the intensity of defiance to a moderate level before imposing discipline.

I hope, as you've read these examples, you haven't become discouraged! To get children to do what they're told to do, we need only choose one of the models we've examined and transform it into a disciplinary command.

In the next chapter, we'll learn to transform any chosen model of discipline into a powerful disciplinary command by using the HoNoR Role. We've already seen the importance of Honesty in devising effective commands. Now we'll tap into Nurturance and hold children Responsible for their behavioral choices.

"Where did we ever get the crazy idea that in order to make children do better, first we have to make them feel worse? Think of the last time you felt humiliated or treated unfairly. Did you feel like cooperating or doing better?"— Jane Nelsen

Chapter Five

Making discipline work (without going to jail)

Word language telling children what to do is merely an expression of wishes unless it's followed by consequences. Word language is transformed into powerful commands by action language. Discipline consists of word language *linked* to "honest" action language consequences. Mere wishes, expressed as word language, but disconnected from consequences, are not discipline. Nor is discipline word language in conflict with stated consequences. Children ignore both forms of verbal expression.

Effective discipline requires children to experience word language honestly predicting consequences. Children rely on the consequences they experience. They know intuitively this is critical for their survival. Children follow honest commands and ignore dishonest commands. People often ask, "How can we get children to do what we tell them to do?" The answer is: By presenting honest word language commands. In the last chapter we saw three children recognize and ignore dishonest word language commands.

While the first requirement of the HoNoR Role is Honesty in predicting the consequences of children's behavior, the second requirement is Nurturance, which you recall consists of love and affection. Within the realm of nurturance lie action language consequences so powerful they overwhelm all competing defiant goals. When nurturance is used to activate discipline, children are compelled to do what you tell them to do. Let's look more closely at nurturance.

Nurturance: A series of acts

All things parents do to raise children are nurturance. Children need nurturance to grow. By providing more of it over a longer period of time than anyone else, parents influence children's growth more powerfully than any other authorities. One part of nurturance – food, shelter and clothing - is necessary under all circumstances for children to survive. Another part of nurturance is not life sustaining, but simply enjoyable. These "required" and "optional" parts of nurturance are Love and Affection. Their relationship is diagrammed below.

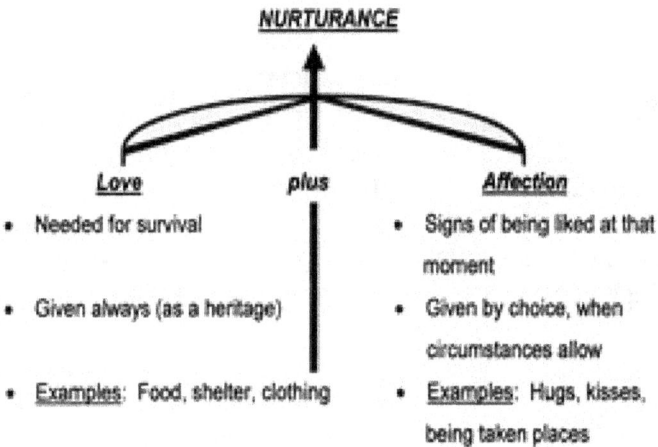

NURTURANCE

Love plus **Affection**

- Needed for survival
- Given always (as a heritage)
- Examples: Food, shelter, clothing

- Signs of being liked at that moment
- Given by choice, when circumstances allow
- Examples: Hugs, kisses, being taken places

About Love

Love is the life-sustaining part of nurturance. To be an effective part of children's environment, that is, to have any active influence on children's growth, love must "speak" in action language. This means love is experienced through a series of actions. The most basic action language of love is the consistent provision of food, shelter and clothing, "no strings attached." Another definition of love is "being there when it counts."

Love is a heritage, completely independent of behavior (or misbehavior). No matter how obnoxious misbehavior becomes, parents don't have the right to deny love to their children. Even when they cannot themselves provide food, shelter or clothing, parents have a duty to provide those "loving" essentials of life through other individuals or agencies. Failure to do so defines parental neglect.

Since love is perceived only through its consequences, it must be considered a series of acts rather than a feeling. Loving children is best viewed as hard work rather than a strong emotion. Telling children they're loved is a non-event. Without consequences, the words are merely wishes to love. They are meaningless, dishonest and (justifiably) ignored.

Because children perceive love through its consequences, denying food, shelter or clothing translates into withdrawal of the survival part of nurturance. This creates immediate panic for children and leads to major misbehavior. Parents must never deny or threaten to deny love to control defiance.

Besides being necessary for children's survival, love magnifies the workings of affection, the "optional" part of nurturance.

About Affection

Affection is what's given when any caretaker or authority appropriately hugs, kisses, touches, holds, takes children places or buys them things. It's the sauce on the meat of love. Affection alone can't sustain life, but like spice in a nutritious meal, it can create a hearty appetite; the motivation for right behavior.

Unlike love, affection is not a heritage. It can be offered or denied to children by any caretaker or authority as a matter of choice. Like any other part of the environment, children perceive affection as a series of acts, not as feelings. "Feelings" of affection by a caretaker are merely wishes to act affectionately. Acts of affection "speak" in action language. When caretakers choose to act affectionately, their actions are saying, "We are pleased with your behavior and we are enjoying your presence."When caretakers choose to withhold affection as a consequence of misbehavior, such acts "speak" of displeasure with the child's behavior.

In the case of parents or guardians, affection is transformed into an even more powerful "super" force capable of energizing discipline and propelling children toward right behavior.

Affection within Love relationships: "Superaffection"

Parents and other guardians of children devote much of their lives to the work of love, which is why within such relationships affection is stronger than it is from any other sources. We might call affection "supercharged" with love, Superaffection.

Just like affection, Superaffection can be offered or denied to children as a consequence of their behavior and as a matter of choice.

Superaffection creates incredibly powerful action language. For parents and others who care for children within love relationships, Superaffection has several characteristics which make it ideal for disciplining defiant children.

Superaffection: Given as a reward, denied as a punishment

- Overpowers all other action language from the environment.

- Can't be "taken" unless parents choose to give it.

- Costs little or nothing.

- Can be used to empower discipline.

If we glance back at the four models of discipline in the last chapter, we'll see that each uses either punishment, reward or both to repel or attract children to right behavior. Although almost any punishment or reward could be used to energize disciplinary commands, the most powerful, most effective and most easily controlled action language consequence for parents is the giving or withholding of Superaffection.

The thought of withholding affection from children creates guilt and impotence in the face of defiance for those parents or caretakers who fail to distinguish between love and affection. The answers to questions directed at the first two requirements of the HoNoR role will lead you away from this trap:

Question #1: How can we get children to do what we tell them to do?

Answer: By using honest forms of discipline. By "honest" we mean word language must accurately and consistently predict consequences.

Question #2: (This is asked by those who confuse love and affection.) Will children know they're loved if they're denied Superaffection?

Answer: Yes, if they're consistently provided with love, the "survival" part of nurturance.

Nurture with Love; Discipline honestly with (Super)Affection

Within a loving relationship, affection becomes "supercharged." Like affection, Superaffection can be denied by choice without diminishing, or even threatening, love.

Superaffection is action language. Whenever it's offered, it says, "I like being with you and I like what you're doing." Using affection honestly means offering it consistently to express pleasure with right behavior and withholding it consistently to indicate displeasure with misbehavior. Consistently withholding affection in the presence of misbehavior meets the test of honesty. Doing otherwise is a misuse of affection and (dishonestly) expresses pleasure with misbehavior and encourages even more of it.

Parents don't have to act affectionately to love children. If they're there when it counts, providing food, shelter and clothing as a heritage, no matter how obnoxious defiance may be and how much (Super)affection they must withhold as a consequence, they're acting lovingly. Children understand the love part of nurturance through these acts alone. The heritage of love doesn't depend on affection for its existence or perception.

Let's look at two examples of discipline energized with Superaffection in the Billiard and Hansel & Gretel modes.

Linda's a pain in the neck; Mom disciplines her in the Billiard Mode

Linda is five years old and her Mom has to wear a neck brace. Mom will have to wear the brace for three months. As of late, Linda has begun to cling to Mom whenever she's told to do something she doesn't want to do. This results in physical pain and mental anguish for Mom. She gets angry at Linda because she causes her pain in the neck, but she feels guilty pushing Linda away because she fears Linda won't know she's loved.

One day, Mom and Linda visit a psychologist. He watches Linda's moderate defiance until Mommy breaks into tears. He suggests a simple solution. Mom will put a star chart in Linda's room with a box drawn on it for each day of the week. Linda is given two stars each morning to keep in her pocket. Whenever she hangs on Mom and whines to be carried, Mom takes one of her stars away. At bedtime, Linda pastes any remaining stars on the chart in the day's box. If she has a star at bedtime, Linda hears a bedtime story. Otherwise, she goes right to bed. Linda is told Mom will be going to the zoo on the weekend, but Linda may go only if she has a star in each box that week. If even one box is empty by the weekend, Linda will stay at home with a babysitter, while Mom will go out alone. Mom is unsure she'll be able to deny Linda a trip to the zoo if she doesn't stop her defiance, but the pain in her neck and the psychologist's reassurance compel her to try.

Mom and Linda return to the psychologist three weeks later. Mom relates Linda didn't seem to respond to this plan the first week. Linda kept no stars. Following the psychologist's advice, Mom managed to have Linda stay home with a babysitter while she went out herself. The second week, Linda filled all her boxes with stars. She didn't whine and she asked to be carried only once. This week, several times a day, Linda proudly announces to her Mom she's "not asking to be carried." She waits until Mom responds with a hug. Linda is very happy and Mom no longer has a pain in her neck.

Discussion: Linda's misguided (and painful for Mom) defiant goal is to be held and carried. At first, Mom confuses affection and love. She feels guilty about pushing Linda away because she doesn't distinguish between the affectionate act of holding Linda and the loving acts of providing Linda a home and being there when it counts.

The psychologist helps Mom design and activate a disciplinary command in the Billiard mode to end Linda's defiance. Mom's Superaffection is chosen to transform the model into a command. The punishment, "staying home with the babysitter" is used to block the defiance while two rewards, "Mom will read a bedtime story" and "You can come with me to the zoo" are chosen to deflect (like a billiard ball) Linda's defiant goal of hanging on Mom.

Here's a diagram showing how the Billiard mode of discipline is transformed to a powerful command using Mom's Superaffection: (See next page.)

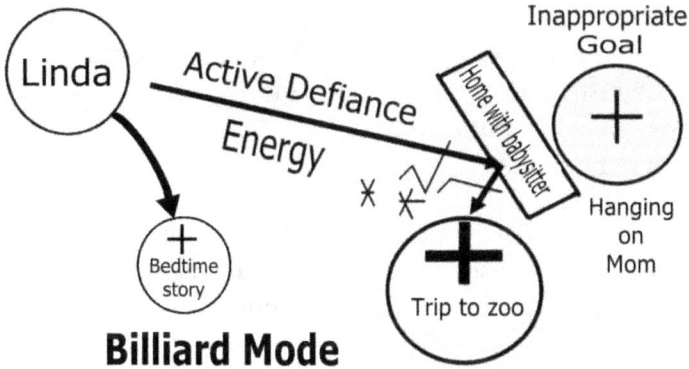

Billiard Mode

In the diagram of discipline in Billiard mode we examined in Chapter Four, only one reward was shown. Here, because Linda is young, immediate and delayed rewards are used to insure early success (with immediate relief for Mom!) and continued right behavior.

A star chart is a useful "pegboard" on which to hang disciplinary commands for preschoolers and elementary schoolers. The stars provide incremental reminders to young children of their progress toward rewarding goals or looming punishment if their defiance continues. In the example above, the stars are encouragement for Linda to continue working for a bedtime story. The bedtime story, in turn, becomes an even greater attraction for continued right behavior, ultimately leading to a trip to the zoo.

For older, more mature children who are able to work for long-term goals, written contracts can serve as pegboards on which to hang disciplinary commands. Both star charts and written contracts allow parents to arrange rewards in progressively more powerful sequences to lure children toward distant goals. These motivational techniques and several others are discussed in greater detail in Appendix II.

Children's perceptions of love and Superaffection, the components of parents' nurturance, are different for fathers and mothers and at different stages of children's lives. This situation is exaggerated in divorce, where the custodial parent has more powerful Superaffection available to activate word language commands. To successfully control moderate defiance, and especially to promote right behavior, the custodial parent(s) must "lend" Superaffection to the other parent or parents.

Here's an example of discipline in the Hansel and Gretel mode imposed on a teenager. Though her parents are divorced, they are able to cooperate and share Superaffection to manage their daughter's misbehavior.

Mom's Superaffection helps Dad Entice Sarah to better asthma control

Sarah, 14-years-old, has asthma and lives with her mother. Her parents are divorced and her father is remarried. Sarah complains she doesn't like her stepmother (Dad's new wife) because "she has too many rules."

Sarah's asthma requires the regular use of inhalers to avoid wheezing. She's very good about taking her medicines at Mom's home and in school. But when Sarah visits Dad and his wife, she often "forgets" to take her medication. This results in wheezing severe enough to shorten her visits with Dad. As hard as they've tried, Dad and his wife haven't been able to get Sarah to take her medicines regularly.

Dad asks his pediatrician for help on one of Sarah's trips to the doctor's office. Sarah, her Stepmom and her Dad meet with the doctor. She determines Sarah's Dad and his wife are truly loving parents, but Sarah spends only four weeks each year with them. Although Sarah's Dad is there when it counts and provides for Sarah's needs for the month she visits, Sarah sees her mother as more "loving" than her father because her mother provides the "survival" part of nurturance for eleven months of the year. Dad and Stepmom's affection is not powerful enough to compete with the Superaffection Sarah anticipates getting from Mom upon returning home.

Sarah's failure to use her asthma inhalers is an example of passive defiance. As we learned in Chapter Four, passive defiance is best managed with rewards in the Hansel and Gretel mode of discipline. "Splattering" Sarah's misbehavior against punishments with the Brick Wall or Billiard forms of discipline will likely create anger or depression. Such feelings on Sarah's part would only worsen her relationship with her Stepmom. But where can one find powerful enough rewards to empower Hansel and Gretel discipline?

After a conference call with Mom and the family, the pediatrician designs a word language command in Hansel and Gretel (rewards in sequence) mode to entice Sarah to control her asthma when she's with her Dad.

Chosen as immediate rewards are easing up on two rules by Stepmom all agree aren't required for children of Sarah's age (e.g. - going to bed at 9:00 PM on weekends and saving all her allowance for buying clothes). To make the command more compelling, Superaffection is chosen as a delayed reward; a slumber party arranged by Mom for Sarah when she returns home, if the asthma is controlled while she's with Dad. The details of Sarah's agreement with her family are posted on the refrigerator as a written contract.

Here's a diagram of Sarah's discipline in the Hansel and Gretel mode: (See next page.)

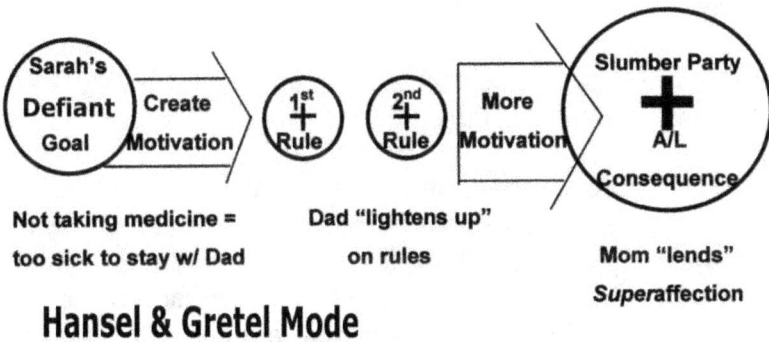

Not taking medicine = too sick to stay w/ Dad

Dad "lightens up" on rules

Mom "lends" Superaffection

Hansel & Gretel Mode

<u>Discussion</u>: In this idealized example, divorced but cooperative parents work together to do what's best for Sarah. In less fortunate cases, where children are caught between warring parents who are uncooperative, only punishments are available and powerful enough for discipline. This leaves the Brick Wall as the sole form of discipline, exclusively requiring punishment. As we've seen, Brick Wall discipline "splatters" children's misbehavior against punishment, causing anger or depression.

Parents who cannot or will not "share" the Superaffection of the custodial parent, and who rely on the Brick Wall mode of discipline, unwittingly intensify their children's anger and depression and so grow moderate misbehavior into more intense misbehavior.

Another question often posed by parents, "Should I offer Superaffection for right behavior and withhold it for misbehavior?" The answer helps define the final requirement of the HoNoR Role as it applies to discipline. The answer, of course, is YES! Experiencing meaningful consequences for right or wrong behavior promotes acceptance of Responsibility, which is the path to adulthood.

Responsibility for Consequences: The last requirement of the HoNoR Role

Being Responsible means accepting the consequences of one's own actions. Adults are directly answerable for their actions. This is different from children. Children depend on adults to take responsibility for their (the children's) misbehavior. For example, when Jimmy swings on the neighbor's gate and breaks it, Mom or Dad, the responsible adults, get the bill.

When children accept responsibility for all their actions, they become adults. This is not an automatic process. Many "grown-ups" are still "children" by this definition. The woman who dissolves into tearful helplessness by the side of the road when her car develops a flat tire is a "grown-up" child. The forty-year-old unemployed man who lives with his parents, occasionally mowing the lawn or taking out the garbage, is another "grown-up" child. These are people who haven't learned to accept responsibility. They depend on others to be responsible for them.

The HoNoR Role is a discipline model designed to create adults out of children. It empowers discipline through the power of nurturance and guides children toward adulthood by holding them responsible for their acts.

Let's revisit the examples of Bobby in the kitchen, Jefferson getting a shot and Debbie becoming an alcoholic. We'll see how the HoNoR Role, used to design all forms of discipline, leads children to accept responsibility for their behavior.

Bobby's in the Kitchen Again: Using the HoNoR Role to Design a Word Language Command

Remember Bobby, the two and a half year old who's watching Mommy ice a cake? In Chapter Four, before she'd learned the HoNoR Role, Mommy screamed, "No! Don't touch it," when Bobby reached for the icing. Mommy's word language was merely a wish and Bobby ignored it.

This time, Mommy creates a word language command in the Billiard mode to deflect Bobby's defiance. She uses the HoNoR Role as a model. As in past examples, rewards and punishments are enclosed within parentheses:

"Bobby, if you sit on the chair to watch me, [you may have some ice cream]; if you touch the cake, [you'll have to go to your room]."

Here's a diagram of Mommy's discipline presented in Billiard mode.

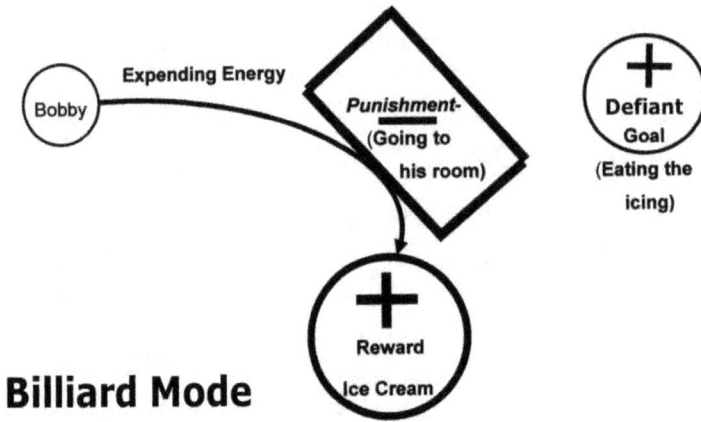

Billiard Mode

Bobby is given an honest word language command. It predicts the punishment for his defiance will be going to his room. Nurturance, by way of Superaffection from Mommy (eating ice cream with her) is the reward for controlling his impulse to touch or eat the cake. Bobby is allowed to make a choice and accept responsibility for the consequences.

Now, see now how Jefferson, the five-year-old getting a shot at the doctor's office, can benefit from his parents' use of the HoNoR Role to design discipline in Distraction mode:

Jefferson gets a shot: His parents use the HoNoR Role to design discipline in the Distraction mode

Mommy and Daddy know five-year-old Jefferson hates shots. Mommy hates them, too, and becomes upset just watching Jefferson get one. They decide to create discipline in Distraction mode using the HoNoR Role. In choosing Distraction as the mode of discipline, the parents realize Jefferson is likely to be angry or depressed after getting his shot. Distraction, using no punishment, is unlikely to intensify anger or depression. Their word language command in

Distraction mode is shown below. As before, rewards are enclosed in parentheses:

"The shot will hurt like a "pinch" and some boys cry a little. Daddy will hold you on his lap. If you stop crying right after the shot, [you can have some ice cream on the way home]; if you don't cry at all, [we'll take you to the zoo]."

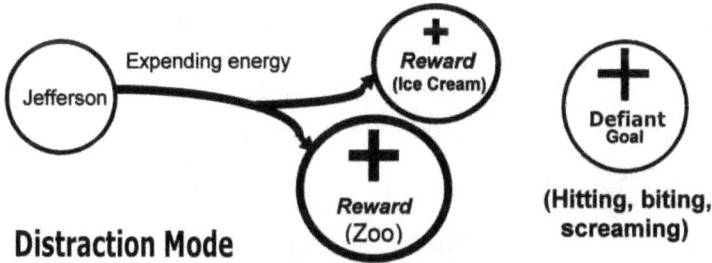

Here's a diagram of this disciplinary command in the Distraction mode.

When the doctor arrives, Mommy greets him warmly, repeats the command and leaves the room. Daddy holds Jefferson on his lap with his son's hands and feet restrained. Jefferson shrieks and struggles as the shot is given, but he's unable to bite, hit or kick either adult.

After the shot is given, Dad hands Jefferson a tissue to dry his tears and reminds him he can have an ice cream if he can stop crying. Later, on the way to the ice cream store, Jefferson asks if they can go to the zoo. Mommy tells Jefferson how proud she is he stopped crying so soon. She indicates he's such a "big boy" the next time he gets a shot he probably won't cry at all and he'll be able to go to the zoo.

Discussion: Mommy is totally honest with Jefferson. She tells him the shot will hurt and predicts the consequences of his behavioral choices. She offers nurturance in the form of Superaffection as rewards (ice cream, going to the zoo). Then she holds Jefferson responsible for the consequences of his acts. She wisely prevents severe defiance by having Daddy restrain Jefferson. She avoids weakening her disciplinary command with the conflicting action language of her own fears by leaving the room.

Jefferson stopped crying after the shot and thus earned his ice cream (the smaller reward); but because he did cry during the shot, he has not honestly earned the greater reward of going to the zoo. Taking him to the zoo after crying would have been dishonest and a bribe.

The HoNoR Role works for older children, too. Here's the case of seventeen-year-old Debbie. You may remember her from Chapter Four as the girl whose mother had forbidden her to drink alcohol and had told her it wasn't good for her. Conflicting action language from the parents, including their drinking without any apparent ill consequences, had made the parents' word language a mere wish, which Debbie ignored.

Debbie is drinking and hoarding beer; The HoNoR Role is used as a template to impose discipline in the Billiard mode

In this example, Debbie's parents use the HoNoR Role to discipline her in the Billiard mode. They target Debbie's beer drinking using the following command. Rewards and punishments are enclosed in parentheses:

"If you continue to act like an alcoholic, with poor grades, diminishing stamina and lost friendships, or if we find more beer cans, we'll have to assume you are an alcoholic, and [we'll have the doctor admit you to the hospital detoxification unit]. If you can get your grades up, stay healthy and resume activities with your friends, and if we find no more evidence of drinking over the next four weeks, [we'll enroll you in Drivers' Education and plan on making a car available to you]."

Here's a diagram of Debbie's parents' word language command in the Billiard mode.

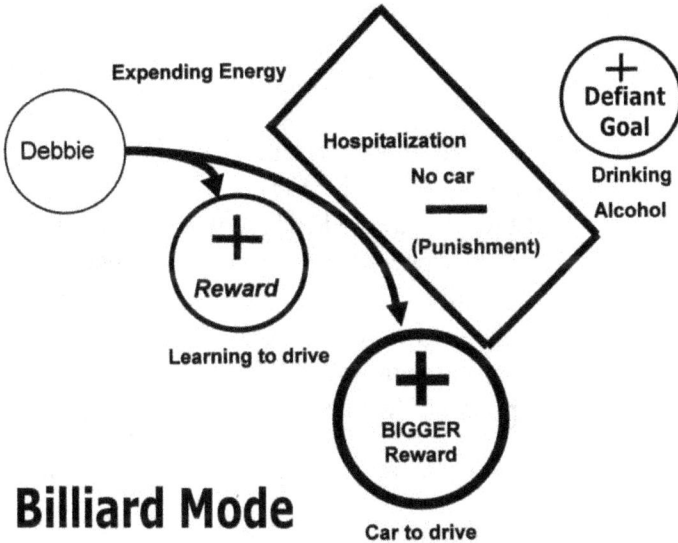

Billiard Mode

Discussion: Debbie's parents recognize the need to stop what appears to be the development of early alcoholism. It's possible Debbie may already be an alcoholic and unable to stop drinking. If that's so, she's exhibiting "hardwired" misbehavior and will need professional help. It's also possible Debbie is choosing to drink to look "grown-up" in the eyes of her friends. In that case, she's choosing to be defiant. One or two degrees more on the misbehavior thermometer will qualify as severe misbehavior and will demand immediate control with overwhelming force through hospitalization. For now, facing moderate misbehavior, there's still time for the parents to plan a strategy, though not a very long time.

Anticipating the possibility of alcoholism, the parents choose hospitalization as the consequence of continued drinking. Debbie will surely see such a consequence as punishment, but the parents are willing to risk the creation of anger or depression to shorten the process of managing their daughter's dangerous misbehavior. To induce her to make better choices if she's (willfully) defiant, they offer Debbie Superaffection. They divide their Superaffection into two sequential rewards; (1) the possibility of learning to drive, as a consequence of immediate cessation of drinking and (2) the availability of a car, for continued abstinence. Offering two "stepped" rewards makes Debbie's success more likely since her first successful effort will be recognized and will intensify her desire to achieve the bigger reward. The parents incorporate these rewards into a discipline command in the Billiard mode.

By using the HoNoR Role to design their discipline command, Debbie's parents offer her an opportunity to take a giant step toward adulthood. Whether Debbie is addicted to alcohol or is willfully choosing to imitate some of her peers by drinking, the consequences of her acts are honestly predicted by her parents' word language command. They nurture her with love, by being there when it counts, even if Debbie is unable to earn Superaffection. And, of course, Debbie is held responsible for her acts.

These examples show how the HoNoR Role is used to create discipline in any of its modes:

- Honest word language predicts the consequences of right or wrong behavior

- Nurturance in the form of (Super)affection is appropriately given or withheld as a reward or a punishment.

- Responsibility is imposed for the child's behavioral choice.

To be effective, forms of affection offered for right behavior must be seen by children as powerful enough to overcome competing rewards for misbehavior. Likewise, affection denied as punishment for misbehavior must be considered important enough to dissuade the child from engaging in further defiance.

Appendix II presents several techniques to enhance the power of rewards and punishments in order to overcome competing chatter from the environment.

Here follows a list of rewards and punishments, arranged in order of increasing intensity, which you'll find useful in designing powerful discipline commands.

Affection And *Superaffection* As *Rewards* And *Punishments*

REWARDS		PUNISHMENTS
Allowing an activity to continue		**Denying or giving some "thing"**
Ex: Watching TV	M	Ex: Passing the ice cream stand
Riding a bicycle	O	Buying nothing at toy store
Play/visit with friends	R	No star for star chart
Driving the family car	E	Withholding allowance
Buying or giving some "thing"		**Restricting an activity**
Ex: Earning a selected toy	P	Ex: No dessert after supper
Establishing an allowance	O	No TV for a defined period
Buy or help to buy a car	W	"Grounded" for a set period
(*Super*)affection as an activity	E	**Isolation from (*Super*)affection**
Ex: Going to a movie with parent(s)	R	Ex: "Go to your room."
Camping trip with parent(s)	F	"Eat in your room alone."
More liberal curfew/rules	U	"Stay home with sitter while
	L	family goes to the zoo."
	L	

Note on the list above, slapping and spanking are conspicuously absent. One reason they've been omitted is only severe misbehavior is managed without regard to the anger or depression which typically follow such punishment. Anger and depression provoke either defiance or withdrawal, making the control of misbehavior more difficult.

Again, Limit Discipline to Moderate, Willful Misbehavior

Remember, don't waste discipline on merely annoying levels of misbehavior or on hardwired or severe misbehavior. Ignore merely annoying behavior, since it's not worthy of your limited energies. And, don't attempt to use rewards or punishments to control hardwired or severe defiance. Rather, STOP severe misbehavior immediately with overwhelming force, if necessary, since it leaves no time for reflection and can kill or maim children or others. For older children, this typically requires the help of medical professionals and/or police.

Finally, remember that before imposing discipline, you must identify, treat or accommodate to any underlying disorders blocking your child's behavioral choice-making.

Only willful defiance at a moderate level is responsive to discipline. This means your child is choosing to misbehave at a level that cannot be ignored, but hasn't reached a crisis point. It means you are sure no underlying physical or mental health condition is keeping your child from choosing right behavior. And, it leaves you time to use the HoNoR Role to safely design a form of discipline.

It's difficult for parents to watch children accept painful or unpleasant consequences, especially if they've been contrived. It's especially hard if parents confuse love and affection. But the alternatives of permitting children to do what they please or protecting them from safe, though unpleasant, consequences of their acts lead away from adulthood, foster continued dependency and threaten love. Often, to defend against such unpleasantness, parents turn to the Professional Idiocy; a belief only professionals know the truth and have the power to manage defiant behavior.

In reality, though professionals assist in diagnosing and managing underlying causes of misbehavior – physical and mental health disorders - parents have the power of Superaffection at their disposal and are best qualified to discipline their children.

The disciplinary schemes presented in this book are powerful tools parents can use for recognizing and disciplining willful misbehavior. Appendices I and II present "Normal" Age Work, and More Motivational Techniques, respectively. These Appendices are presented within the framework you've learned and are meant to be reference materials for deciding if, when and how discipline may be imposed.

Chapter Six

Discipline for dummies: A cheat sheet

This chapter summarizes the essence of the preceding chapters. It will jog your memory as you apply the five steps you've learned:

•Recognize misbehavior.

•Judge its severity and STOP life-endangering levels while ignoring merely annoying levels.

•Diagnose and treat (with professional help) misbehavior your child can't control.

•Design an effective form of discipline for the remaining defiance.

•Impose the chosen form of discipline (without going to jail).

At the end of the chapter you will find a cheat sheet you can use to apply these steps to any form of misbehavior you encounter. Let's begin with the recognition of misbehavior.

Recognizing misbehavior – Chapter One

Misbehavior in a child is recognized by its destructive effect on critical life functions. The injurious consequences of misbehavior interfere with a child's ability to use its body and mind at a level expected for its age (physical, social, communication skills, which we've named Age Work). The consequences of misbehavior may also prevent a child from following reasonable rules (Authority relationships). Finally, the consequences of misbehavior threaten relationships to Others, generating a pattern of complaints from Others. These targets of misbehavior - Age

Work, Authority and Others - we've called the Consequence Areas.

Any deficiency in the Consequence Areas of Age Work (including its subdivisions of physical, social or communication skills), Authority relationships or relationships with Others qualifies as misbehavior.

Whether something need be done about the misbehavior and how quickly (if at all) it must be done is determined by the severity of the misbehavior.

Judging the severity of misbehavior – Chapter Two

There are two measures of severity of misbehavior in children. Deficiencies in the Consequence Areas are objective measures of misbehavior and we can count the number of Consequence Areas affected by any suspect behavior. The more areas affected, the greater the severity of the misbehavior.

The second measure of severity of misbehavior is the intensity of the emotional reaction generated in the observer (e.g.- parent, guardian or caretaker). The more intense the emotional reaction, the more intense the misbehavior. Typical emotions experienced by the observers of misbehavior in children, in increasing levels of intensity, include: annoyance, Confusion, Anxiety or Anger and FEAR.

It's possible to assign scores to each Consequence Area threatened by a child's misbehavior and the sum of these scores provide an objective measure of severity. We can also assign a score to any of three levels of emotional reaction experienced by observers of misbehavior (mild, Moderate, SEVERE). This score provides a subjective measure of severity.

Combining the objective and the subjective scores provides an accurate measure of the severity of any misbehavior.

How we derive the objective score

Each of the three subdivisions of Age Work (physical, social and communication) carries 1 point for a possible total of 3 points if all three skill areas are threatened.

The Consequence Area of Others consists of Parents and Everyone Else. Behavior targeting parents generates 1 point and that targeting anyone else generates another point for a possible total of 2 points.

Threats to Authority, including parents, teachers, (peers and siblings, if in authority) or anyone else in authority generate 1 point.

Thus, the maximum number of objective points generated by misbehavior may total 6.

How we derive the subjective score

Emotional reactions experienced by observers of misbehavior may be divided into mild, Moderate or SEVERE levels. Mere annoyance is considered a mild reaction. Anxiety, Confusion or Anger are considered moderate reactions. FEAR is considered a severe reaction.

In scoring subjective reactions, a mild response is given 1 point. Moderate reactions are given 2 points. SEVERE reactions are given 3 points. For any observed misbehavior, only the most intense reaction is scored.

Thus the maximum number of subjective points generated by misbehavior is 3 points.

What to do with the combined misbehavior score

Combining objective and subjective scores accurately defines the intensity and potential for life-endangerment of any misbehavior.

Scores of 7 – 9 points define potentially life-endangering misbehavior requiring IMMEDIATE control with overwhelming force, if required. There is no time to determine causes or to develop strategies for persuading the child to stop misbehaving.

•A 911 call may be required for law enforcement assistance, especially with combative teens.

•Immediate psychiatric hospitalization may be required to lower the level of potential danger created by the misbehavior.

•The short-term goal for parents facing SEVERE misbehavior is to lower the level of intensity of the misbehavior to the point where causes for the misbehavior may then be sought and where strategies may be developed (including discipline) to guide the child toward right behavior.

Scores of 3, 4, 5 or 6 points define Moderate levels of misbehavior. Misbehavior at this level requires attention, but leaves time for parents to discover causes, including underlying physical and mental health disorders. Some of these conditions (like ADHD, Bipolar Disorder, Cerebral Palsy, Developmental Delay or Epilepsy) will require professional assistance to diagnose and treat while others may require parents to accept and live with the associated behaviors.

Scores of 1 and 2 points define merely annoying (trivial) misbehavior. I advise parents to ignore this level of misbehavior and focus on Moderate levels of misbehavior, once SEVERE levels have been downgraded.

Once misbehavior has been limited to the Moderate level by downgrading SEVERE forms and ignoring mild forms, focus can be turned to finding any underlying physical or mental health conditions ontributing to the misbehavior and not under the child's control. This step is critical because misbehavior not under a child's control cannot respond to discipline.

Find disorders not under the child's control – Chapter Three

Willful disobedience "looks" and "feels" different from misbehavior not under a child's control. Misbehavior caused by disorders not under a child's control might be called "hardwired" misbehavior. Here's the look and feel of such behavior:

Hardwired Misbehavior – Its Look and Feel

What It Looks Like (Your observation)	What It Feels Like (Your emotional reaction)
The misbehavior doesn't make sense	
• It happens unpredictably	
	Confusion
• It targets everyone (non-selective)	
.............................and/or..	
There's no benefit to the child	Anxiety
It threatens or hurts the child	

By contrast, defiant misbehavior, where children are choosing to break rules by either doing things they're not supposed to do or not doing things they are supposed to do, looks and feels like this:

Oppositional-Defiant Misbehavior–its look & feel

What It Looks Like (Your observation)	*What It Feels Like* (Your emotional reaction)
The misbehavior is manipulative	*annoyance*
• It's *predictable*.	
• It's *selective*, targeting some people, not others.	
...............................and/or............................	
• It *challenges Authority*, forcing someone to do or allow something unacceptable.	*Anger*

When you suspect a physical or mental health disorder causing hardwired misbehavior which your child can't seem to control, you'll need to get professional help to diagnose and treat any such condition. I suggest you choose professional consultants by checking the subdivisions of Age Work and employing professionals in this order:

- When *physical* skills are lagging, choose a physician.

- When *social* skills are deficient, choose a psychologist.

- When *communication* skills are inadequate, choose an educator.

When two or more areas of Age Work are affected by hardwired misbehavior choose professionals in this order:

Physician > Psychologist > Educator

Once you've identified and treated or eliminated any underlying conditions your child cannot control and which are causing misbehavior, any remaining defiant behavior will respond to discipline.

If you're a parent, you'll want not only to control misbehavior, but also to guide your child toward adulthood.

Choosing an appropriate form of discipline – Chapter Four

Four models of discipline are useful for designing effective discipline for willful defiance. Depending upon the energy your child devotes to misbehavior, different forms of discipline may be chosen.

For children who are actively misbehaving; that is, choosing to do things they're not supposed to do, three forms of discipline may be used. One form, the Brick Wall model, blocks defiance with a punishment. This form of discipline often causes the child to become angry or depressed. Though it is the fastest-working form of discipline, it does not guide the child toward right behavior and may intensify misbehavior. It is diagrammed below:

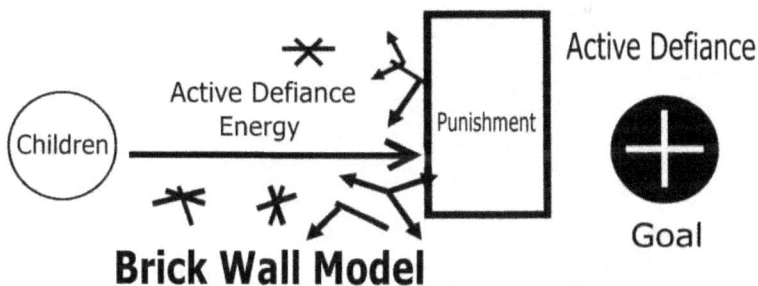

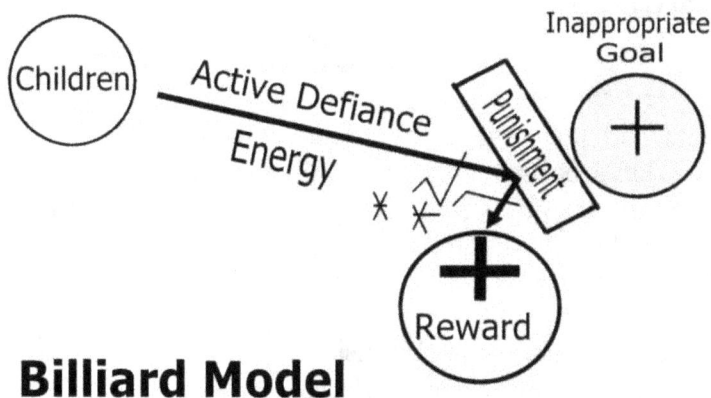

Brick Wall Model

Billiard Model

A second form of discipline, the Billiard model, uses punishment to block misbehavior while a reward is used to redirect the misbehavior toward right behavior. This model, like the Brick Wall mode, works fast, but results in less anger or depression in the child. Choosing effective rewards takes more time and thought than choosing punishments. The Billiard mode of discipline is diagrammed above:

This form of discipline does guide a child toward right behavior.

A third form of discipline, the Distraction model, distracts a child from misbehavior by offering two or more rewards together for right behavior. This form of discipline can be used to redirect active defiance, where a child is expending energy doing things it's not supposed to do. Because it uses no punishment, no anger or depression results from this model. Additionally, the Distraction mode may be used for passive defiance, where a child is failing to do things it's supposed to be doing.

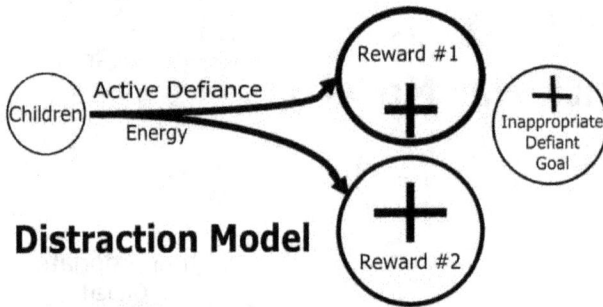

This model, and the Hansel and Gretel model to follow, require more thought and planning to be effective than discipline using punishment. That's because different children respond to different rewards. Parents are the best designers of discipline in the Distraction and Hansel and Gretel modes because they can choose the most effective rewards for such discipline.

The fourth model of discipline to consider is the Hansel and Gretel mode. In this model, rewards are offered in sequence – one after another – to lure a defiant child toward right behavior. Beside its ability to redirect misbehavior toward right behavior in children who are actively defiant, this form of discipline can motivate an otherwise unmotivated child to do things it's been choosing not to do – like completing homework or raising failing grades. This form of discipline is diagrammed below:

After choosing an appropriate form of discipline for Moderately defiant behavior – either active or passive – parents must activate

Hansel & Gretel Model

the model with powerful punishments, rewards or both. But parents must do more than merely stop misbehavior. They must guide their children toward adulthood.

Making discipline work (without going to jail) – Chapter Five

Each of the discipline models you've seen require either punishments or rewards powerful enough to overcome your child's anticipated "reward" for defiance. Within the nurturing relationship parents share with their children may be found love and affection. Love is a child's heritage, independent of behavior. Affection is a series of acts offered to a child as evidence of pleasure with and acceptance of that child's behavior. Within a love relationship, like that of parents and their children, affection is more intense than that offered by other caretakers or authorities. We've called affection within love relationships Superaffection.

Superaffection, when offered as a reward, is more powerful than any other bounty. When it is denied, it is a most powerful form of punishment. In order to use Superaffection to empower discipline, parents must remember love (food, shelter and clothing – being there when it counts – fostering healthy growth) is unaffected by withholding affection (acts by a parent attesting to right behavior).

Offering Superaffection to a defiant child translates to, "I accept and approve of your misbehavior". Such acts by parents are dishonest forms of communication and equivalent to bribery. They inevitably encourage more misbehavior.

In order to design and empower effective forms of discipline to redirect defiance and guide children toward adulthood, parents should follow the HoNoR Role:

●Honestly predict the consequences of misbehavior and right behavior in any form of discipline.

●Nurture your child with love, but withhold Superaffection as punishment for defiance and offer it as a reward for right acts.

●Allow your child to accept Responsibility for behavioral choices along with predicted consequences.

To make it easy to apply the principles you've learned in this book, use the cheat sheet that follows.

Disciplining Your Child

1 — What's worrying you?

Write in the behavior you're concerned about:

[   ]

Does it threaten any *Consequence Area?*

Check any boxes affected:

- Authority.......
- Others.........
  - Physical
  - Social
  - Communication
- Age Work

(diagram: Phy / Soc / Comm)

IGNORE if no boxes √'d.

If *any* √'s, it's Misbehavior. Go to *STEP 2*

2 — Score the Objective boxes you checked in Step 1:

- Authority (anyone's) = 1 pt
- Others complaining — You = 1 pt / Anyone else = 1 pt
- Age Work: Phy=1 /Soc=1/Comm=1 - Up to 3 pts

Now score the Subjective criteria - only your most intense reaction:

- annoyance = 1 pt
- Anger, Confusion or Anxiety = 2 pts
- FEAR = 3 pts

+ =

- *annoying* = 1–2 pts → Ignore
- *Moderate* = 3–6 pts → *Go to Step 3*
- *SEVERE* = 7–9 pts → *STOP* with whatever means are required!

3 — Discover and treat underlying physical or mental disorders:

"Hardwired" looks & feels →
- Non-selective (Targets anyone, anywhere)
- No benefit (Achieves nothing for the kid)
- Random timing (Occurs anytime)

→ You will need professional help: Physician → Psychologist → Educator
- Be sure to proceed in this order.

or

Defiant looks & feels →
- Selective (Only some people, some places)
- Achieves inappropriate goals
- Predictable timing

→ Go on to Step 4

4 — Choose a form of discipline: (remember, until activated, all forms of discipline are merely suggestions!)

- Rock Wall: *"Stop or else"* Advantages: Fast; only 1 consequence. Dis.: Wastes child's energy, can "splatter" anger!
- Billiard: *"Stop or else : do this & (reward)"* Fast, saves child's energy Dis.: More work, some anger, depression
- Distraction: *"Do this & (reward); or that & (reward)"* Adv.: No anger, saves energy Dis.: Takes time, complicated
- Hansel & Gretel: *"Do this & (reward), continue & (reward)"* Adv: Motivates w/o anger, but takes time & thought.

5 — Now, *Activate* the discipline you chose in Step 4 with Superaffection while following the HoNoR Role:

- H – Be Honest by doing what you say you'll do.
- N – Nurture with love; use Superaffection (either offered or denied) as rewards or punishment.
- R – Hold your children Responsible for the consequences of their behavioral choices.

Appendix I
Critical Markers for Age Work

In the first three chapters of this book, you learned to:

•Identify defiant behavior - *Chapter One*

•Determine the intensity of misbehavior, STOP severe forms and ignore trivial forms.- *Chapter Two*

•Identify and manage underlying disorders which steal choice-making.- *Chapter Three*

Underlying physical and mental health disorders may be suspected whenever Age Work is threatened. To eliminate underlying disorders, and with it any barriers to children's free choice-making, parents must be sure their children can meet age-related expectations within the *physical, social,* and *communication* ability areas of Age Work. It isn't necessary to consult a specialist before making this determination. Simple markers in each skill area are sufficient to prompt parents to suspect "hardwired" misbehavior. Only if and when children fail to meet one or more markers of normal Age Work, suggesting the presence of an underlying disorder over which children have no control, would professional assistance be mandatory. Such assistance, you'll recall, follows this path:

Physical delays ⟶ **Physician**

Social delays ⟶ **Psychologist**

Communication delays ⟶ **Educator**

Because underlying disorders present barriers to choice-making, their presence limits children's compliance with discipline. Indeed, some disorders, like Autistic Spectrum Disorders, AD(H)D, Bipolar Disorder, Cerebral Palsy, Developmental and Intellectual Disabilities and Epilepsy, force parents to accept or adjust to certain forms of misbehavior. Eliminating underlying barriers to behavioral choice-making is a critical step to insure success with the imposition of discipline.

Tell Me Again – What Services Must Parents Get From Professionals?

As a parent seeking professional assistance to evaluate delays in Age Work, you must specifically request answers to these questions:

- What are the possible causes of the delay and how will they be identified or eliminated?

- Will any of the possible causes of the delay result in a leveling off or even a loss of progress and if that happens, how will it be recognized?

- At what level is my child currently functioning and how far from normal is the level now?

- What tests will be used to track progress and how often will they be administered?

Any professional who cannot or will not answer these questions in a direct and easily understood fashion is the wrong expert for you.

Here follows a table of expected abilities for various age ranges in each of the skill areas of Age Work. It presents normal achievement levels for body health, social, and communication skills which I've observed and found useful over many years of practice. These markers are not meant to be used as a sole measure of intelligence or developmental age. They are presented to allow you to recognize delays in Age Work pointing to possible underlying physical or mental health disorders. Such delays, if unrecognized, will block successful discipline. Remember the "look" and "feel" of hardwired misbehavior:

The table that follows is a reference you can use to quickly check for delays in Age Work, the origins of hardwired misbehavior.

Hardwired Misbehavior – Its Look and Feel

What It Looks Like (Your observation)	What It Feels Like (Your emotional reaction)
The misbehavior doesn't make sense	
• It happens unpredictably	
	Confusion
• It targets everyone (non-selective)	
....and/or...	
There's no benefit to the child	Anxiety
It threatens or hurts the child	

Markers of Age Work for Various Ages
(See tables on pages 119 and 120.)

To use this table, find the appropriate age range for your child and see if the listed markers are met for *physical, social,* and *communication* abilities for that age range. If so, underlying disorders are unlikely and your child is *capable* of choosing right behavior. If not, your child will need evaluation, diagnosis and possible treatment for underlying disorders. Sometimes, for certain medical or mental health conditions, parents may discover they'll have to limit their expectations accordingly.

Markers of *Age Work* For Various Age Ranges[1,2]

Note: Markers for Age Work are coded to indicate which professionals to consult first if delays are suspected-

"ᗅ" *Physician*   "♥" *Psychologist*   "ᚾ" *Educator*

	Physical	Social	Communication
Newborn Baby	ᗅ Moves all extremities ᗅ Sucks to feed ᗅ Passes urine and stool	ᗅ Able to calm when held and rocked	ᗅ Able to cry loudly
By 3 months	ᗅ Lifts head up when lying on belly ᗅ Able to unclench fists ᗅ Reacts to visual threat	ᗅ Anticipates feeding ᗅ Recognizes parent ᗅ Able to smile	ᗅ Coos "musically"
By 5 months	ᗅ Able to hold rattle ᗅ Can roll over to back	ᗅ Smiles socially	ᗅ Able to babble
By 6 months	ᗅ Sits alone briefly ᗅ Can suck toes ᗅ Transfers objects from one hand to other ᗅ Reaches for objects	ᗅ Recognizes someone is a stranger ᗅ Feeds self ᗅ Searches for toy	ᗅ Turns to voice ᗅ Single syllables
By 8 months	ᗅ Sits without support	ᗅ Laughs in playful situations	ᗅ Able to say "da", "ba"
By 9 – 10 months	ᗅ Able to crawl ᗅ Pulls to standing ᗅ Walks holding on	ᗅ Explores environment ᗅ Plays pat-a-cake ᗅ Indicates wants	ᗅ Understands "No!" ᗅ Says "Mama, Dada" (Non-specific)
By 12 months	ᗅ Stands alone briefly ᗅ Walks alone briefly ᗅ Picks up small objects	♥ Imitates activities ♥ Cooperates with dressing	ᗅ Says "Mama, Dada" (Specific) ᗅ Follows one step commands w/ gesture
By 15 months	ᗅ Creeps up stairs ᗅ Scribbles ᗅ Stacks 2 blocks	ᗅ Drinks from a cup ♥ "Helps" with housework	♥ At least 4 words
By 18 months	ᗅ Runs ᗅ Throws while standing ᗅ Turns pages in a book	♥ Plays alongside other kids ♥ Uses spoon and fork	♥ Knows 5 body parts ♥ Knows at least 6 words

Markers of Age Work For Various Age Ranges [1,2] (Continued)

Note: Markers for Age Work are coded to indicate which professionals to consult first if delays are suspected-

"♭" Physician   "♥" Psychologist   "♫" Educator

	Physical	Social	Communication
By 2 years age	▶ Walks up & down stairs without help ▶ Can partially undress ▶ Imitates pencil strokes	▶ Brushes teeth with help ▶ Imitates washing and drying hands ▷ Anticipates toileting needs	▶ Uses 2 word phrases ▶ Uses pronouns (I, you, me) *inappropriately* ▶ Follows 2 step commands
By 3 years age	▷ Alternates feet when climbing stairs ▷ Can peddle a tricycle ▼ Copies a circle	▶ Knows name and gender ▶ Shares toys ▷ Washes hands	▶ 3 word phrases ▶ Uses pronouns *appropriately* ▶ Uses plurals
By 4 years age	▷ Hops, skips, alternates feet going *down* stairs ▷ Buttons clothes ▼ Copies a square	▶ Plays *cooperatively* with other kids ▶ Dresses without help	▷+▼ Knows colors ♫ Asks questions ♫ Speech understandable to *everyone*
By 5 years age	▷ Able to balance briefly on 1 foot ▷ Adequate stamina for preschool or K ▼ Able to draw a stick figure of a person	▶ Plays competitively ▶ Abides by rules ▶ Helps with household chores	♫ Prints 1st name ♫ Asks meaning of words ♫ Understands opposites
From 6–12 years	▷ Passes yearly physical exam by Pediatrician ▷ Adequate stamina for daily activities	▶ Able to make friends ▶ Enjoys meeting parents' expectations ▶ Maintains personal hygiene	♫ Achieves within 1 year of grade level in school (for age)
From 13–18 years	▷ Passes yearly physical exam by Pediatrician ▷ Adequate stamina for daily activities	▶ Able to make friends of either sex ▶ Maintains personal hygiene ▶ Controls emotions without threat to Age Work, Others or Authority	♫ Achieves within 1 grade level in school (for age) *AND/OR* ♫ Able to retain a job, if of legal age, attending to schedules & work-related duties

1. Age ranges 1 month through 5 years adapted from Table 8-4 The Harriet Lane Handbook, 16th Edition – Mosby.
2. Age ranges 1 month through 6 years adapted from Denver Developmental Assessment (Denver II) – Univ Colorado Medical School 1990.

*Age ranges 1 month through 5 years adapted from Table 8-4 The Harriet Lane Handbook, 16 Edition – Mosby.

**Age ranges 1 month through 6 years adapted from Denver Developmental Assessment (Denver II) – University of Colorado Medical School, 1990.

CAUTION: For children up to two years of age who were prematurely born, chronological or "real" age must be corrected before it can be used to plot developmental milestones. This is done by subtracting the number of months of prematurity from "real" age. For example:

An eighteen-month-old child was born after thirty weeks of pregnancy.

"Normal" pregnancy	= 40 wks
This child's pregnancy	= 30 wks
Number of weeks premature	= 10 wks
(Divide 10 weeks by 4 to convert weeks to months	= 2.5 months
This toddler's chronological or "real" age	= 18 mos
Number of months prematurity	= -2.5 mos
"Corrected" chronological age	= 15.5 mos

This is the age used to find expected milestones or markers in the table above. After two years of age, this correction is not necessary.

What to do with delays in Age Work if a physician says, "The child will grow out of it?"

When parents have determined their child is severely misbehaving, they must STOP IT IMMEDIATELY, if they can. If they need a professional's assistance and theirs is unwilling to help, *they must find another* professional to assist them. Parents must avoid the Professional Idiocy – parents know their children at least as well as professionals.

If delay is at a trivial level, parents should follow their professional's advice and wait to see if their child outgrows it. If delays in Age Work are confined to the moderate level and are being monitored by the appropriate professionals, parents need to track their child's progress with the experts.

Although most professionals are committed to providing the best possible are, no professional can be as diligent as a loving parent. Limitations imposed by medical insurance, client overload and school budgets can delay or even obstruct the process of monitoring children's progress and the provision of critical services by physicians, psychologists or educators. Parents must track their children's developmental delays so they can judge how well or how poorly interventions are working, whether their children are gaining or losing ground and whether other approaches are needed.

Appendix II

More motivational techniques

Here follow some additional techniques used to promote and reward right behavior. These techniques are useful for the Billiard, Distraction and Hansel and Gretel modes of discipline.

We'll begin with examples of Star Charts.

The Positive Reinforcement Star Chart Technique

The Positive Reinforcement Star Chart technique begins with no stars. Children get stars as successes are achieved. As such, it provides rewards designed to motivate children who are misbehaving by not doing things they're supposed to be doing. The technique lures children to move toward right behavior. This is a good technique to use whenever children are passively misbehaving. You may recall the Hansel and Gretel mode of discipline is designed to lure children toward a reward (and right behavior) and presents no risk of evoking anger.

Younger children, with mental ages between three and ten to twelve years, can't usually visualize or recall goals which are merely spoken or which are achieved over several days or weeks. To make the process of earning rewards for right behavior more concrete and easily understood for these younger children, a visual means of tracking their progress with stars allows them to remain motivated and see their reward getting closer with each success.

Star (or any simple token) charts keep score of children's progress. Drawings or photos of the rewards they are working toward can be pasted onto the last box of the charts so they see what reward lies in store for their success.

Children with mental ages between three and five years usually do best with only one required act per half day (morning vs. afternoon) for each star. For example, a star in the morning and one in the afternoon for not wetting pants. More complexity is usually not well understood. Remember, a star is only a token of success, but it does represent what might be called a "mini-success" and achieving a star should be accompanied by lots of praise to make it feel like a success.

Young children do even better remembering their goal when a reward can be seen, touched, and played with before starting a star chart. A trip to the toy store, where a child can play with the proposed reward briefly, then returning it to the shelf and coming home (accompanied, no doubt, with screaming!) will fix the reward in the child's mind, giving more meaning to the stars leading to the reward. A photo taken in the store with a cell phone, and then pasted to the star chart identifies the actual reward "waiting for you to get your stars."

Young children do best with daily rewards for up to two stars per day. For older children, star charts can have several rows for each of several days. Children with mental ages older than five years may not need a trip to the store and will usually do well talking about the goal, then writing it into the last box on the chart. For example, at age ten, three stars might be required each day for several days to acquire the reward. One star might be given for "being kind to your brother," another for "cleaning your room," and a third for "doing your homework."

The key to success with a star chart is not the stars; it's the choice of the reward capable of motivating the child to perform a difficult task. As we've seen in our examination of Nurturance, money, toys and other such "things," though potentially effective, are not as powerful rewards as affection or, when doled out by a loved one, Superaffection. For example, two stars might be required by the end of the day to eat with the family (Superaffection) instead of eating alone in one's room.

Positive Reinforcement Star Charts allow children to experience rewards until they become "hooked" on their success. This process of drawing children to rewards avoids triggering anger, but it takes a bit longer than somewhat more punitive strategies. Let's look next at the Negative Reinforcement Star Chart.

The Negative Reinforcement Star Chart

Negative Reinforcement Star Charts begin with children having possession of an adequate number of stars to complete a successful day, or sometimes, extra stars. Each defiant episode results in the loss of a star. At the end of specified periods, as for example, AM, then PM, remaining stars are affixed to the chart and new stars are given for the next sequence. Children, when they are "short" of a required number of stars, must work "extra" (perform more right behavior) to earn more stars and get their reward. Usually, children are given stars to carry in a pocket. If the targeted defiance is observed, a warning may be given, after which, if defiance persists, a star is taken away.

The Negative Reinforcement Star Chart presents children with both the opportunity to earn rewards by retaining their stars and the risk of losing their stars and thus their rewards. This dual presentation of a potential reward or punishment will be recognized (from Chapter Four) as the wiring of word language commands in the Billiard mode. The potential punishment of losing a star deflects children's misdirected energy away from anticipated defiant goals and toward desired rewards for right behavior.

You may recall presenting discipline in the Billiard mode is the most efficient way to control moderate, active defiance; that is, situations in which children are actively doing things they're not supposed to do. Though wiring commands in the Billiard mode preserves much of the energy kids devote to misbehavior, the punishment component does evoke some anger which can ricochet back to the caregiver.

An example of a Negative Reinforcement Star Chart for the bullying of siblings.

A four-year-old who bullies his younger sister might be told he will need a morning star and an afternoon star to eat with the family. A chart is posted in his room with the designated open boxes. Stars are given for the child to carry in his pocket. He is advised he needs to keep his stars for the chart "so you can eat with us." If he is seen bullying his sister, he is given a warning, but if it persists, a star is taken from him. At the end of the agreed upon period, stars are affixed to the chart. Open boxes mean eating alone. Such Superaffection denied is an extremely powerful punishment for bullying.

With this technique, parents might begin by estimating how many times each morning and how many times each afternoon their child engages in the targeted misbehavior. In the example above, if the child averages three bullying episodes per half day, three stars might be given in the morning and three in the afternoon. By reducing bullying to two episodes in the morning and two in the evening, the child would retain one star for each half day, representing a degree of success for that day and earning a reward.

The next day, two stars might be given to start each half day, requiring even better control of the bullying. Depending on the type of misbehavior being targeted, the rate at which a parent would reduce the number of beginning stars each day might vary, but the principle is the same; a gradual reduction of the misbehavior over time by risking loss of stars while offering rewards for success. The younger the child, the more important it is to offer a reward for each successful day, since most young children can't conceptualize the big picture.

Negative Reinforcement Star Charts risk creating anger because taking away a star is a direct punishment. Generating anger can work against parents, especially if children already have anger issues. But when anger has not been a major issue, Negative Reinforcement Star Charts can be a most effective means of demonstrating displeasure with specific forms of misbehavior. And when other children are observing, the technique provides concrete examples to them of "loss" which can occur as a result of defiance.

Now, let's examine how parents can magnify the power of Star Chart techniques to their benefit. Parents can control misbehavior by utilizing the power of sibling rivalry, the normal competition between brothers and sisters.

Competitive Sibling-Enhanced Star Charts

Sibling rivalry can be used to powerfully motivate right behavioral efforts, using either Positive or Negative Reinforcement Star Charts. The technique can be imposed on one of two or more siblings who are misbehaving, using the other siblings who are right behaving as the standards to be met. When all the siblings are engaged in misbehavior, a designated number of stars may be required for any of the children to capture a reward. In the examples to follow, Star Charts provide a means of measuring and acknowledging right behavior. The competing siblings are motivated by sibling rivalry to overwhelm their inappropriate goals with more coercive rewards.

This technique is so powerful and the withdrawal of Superaffection so painful for some parents to watch, that parents who forget the distinction between love and affection are often completely immobilized and unable to effectively utilize the technique. It's worthwhile to remind such parents of the intricacies of love and affection as presented in Chapter Five. Specifically, the heritage of love is given to children no matter if they are misbehaving or right behaving, but the gift of affection (Superaffection, in the case of a love relationship) is only doled out as a reward for right behavior and, to maintain an honest relationship, withheld when it is undeserved by acts of defiance. Honesty, parents must recall, along with Nurturance and the imposition of Responsibility comprise the HoNoR Role, a roadmap for parents to grow children into successful adults.

To fulfill the HoNoR Role while using Competitive Sibling-Enhanced Star Charts, "the stars must fall where they may" giving the siblings an Honest appraisal of their success in compliance,

Nurturance, in the form of affection (or Superaffection) as a reward for their achievement and the opportunity to accept Responsibility for the consequences they've either earned or not earned.

An example of a Competitive Sibling-Enhanced Star Chart:

Consider two sisters, aged four and six years. The six-year-old is fully toilet trained and the four-year-old intentionally urinates in her clothes, though the parents know she can tell when she needs to urinate. Indeed, she tells her parents when she needs to go, then says, "No!" and wets herself when they ask her to go to the bathroom.

The parents set up a Competitive Sibling-Enhanced Star Chart in the Negative Reinforcement mode. Both sisters are given a star to carry. They are brought to a toy store where each girl chooses a toy as a reward for success, then replaces it on the shelf. At home, a chart is posted with one box for each girl for each day. They are advised "anyone who pees in her clothes will lose her star." At day's end, "Everyone with a star goes back to store and gets their toy." If younger sister wets her clothes, her star is taken and, at day's end, both girls go to the store, but only the older sister gets a toy.

It's likely younger sister will come home crying. But, the parents explain, "We'll do the same thing tomorrow." This powerful technique will usually solve the defiance problem within a day or two.

There are variations on this theme. For example, no siblings are required, as shown next.

Competitive Adult-Enhanced Star Charts

Dads and Moms can participate in what could be called Competitive Adult-Enhanced Star Charts. Indeed, the whole family can participate with children of various ages for different age-related rewards. With these Star Charts it's critical to choose powerful rewards to properly motivate each participant. Star Charts can span days, weeks, even months once all participants are engaged in the process.

As an example, using the vignette presented above, except substituting Mom or Dad for the older sibling, the four year old "wetter" can compete with one or more parents for the toy. Since the parents won't likely lose their stars by wetting their clothes, they will take their daughter to the store to watch them claim toys while she observes. In one or two days, the four year old is likely to comply.

Another useful technique, though for older children (ten to twelve, up through young adulthood), is Behavioral Contracting.

Behavioral Contracting – Basic Principles

Behavioral Contracting is a useful technique for older children (usually ten to twelve years of age or older) who can be motivated to achieve a set goal. It's also a way of substituting a powerful, child-oriented goal for an "adult" goal a child does NOT find intrinsically attractive. For example, many children don't find the goal of achieving high grades in school in order to get a higher paying job later attractive enough to motivate them. But, achieving high grades in school to get a dirt bike may be immensely more appealing! Behavioral contracting is an effective way to structure this type of goal modification so:

•There is no confusion about the goal which has been agreed upon

•This means the goal must be precisely defined.

•In the example above, the goal would be higher grades, but specifically "B-level or above" might be required

•There is no confusion about the time frame required to reach the goal.

In the example above, "on your next report card" might be the time frame.

•There is no confusion about the reward for achieving the goal.

•The dirt bike in the example above might be a model examined and mutually agreed upon before completing the contract.

Behavioral contracting is much like the Positive Reinforcement Star Chart you read about earlier, except older children don't need the token stars to remind them each step of the way as they work toward a goal. Both techniques may be designed in the Billiard, Distraction or Hansel and Gretel modes of discipline. The Billiard mode is most effective for children who are doing things they're not supposed to do, while the Distraction and Hansel and Gretel modes are more effective for those who aren't doing things they are supposed to do.

Behavioral contracts need to be written out, with a copy for the parent and one for the child to avoid arguments later. Indeed, one of the most common complaints children direct at parents (and one to avoid if you want to retain credibility) is, "You didn't keep your promise!"

Let's examine some ways to structure behavioral contracts.

Behavioral Contracting for One-Time Goals

Imagine Devon, aged 12 years, is a seventh grade student who has always gotten average grades in his major subjects in school. In past years, Devon stayed home from school very infrequently and only when ill.

Three months ago, Devon's Dad was lost to a heart attack and Devon's Mom became a single parent. The many difficult adjustments imposed on the family resulted in depression for both Mom and Devon, for which each required psychiatric care and medication. Both have made considerable progress in dealing with their loss. Devon's therapist has determined Devon fears something will happen to his Mom at home while he's in school.

Devon has visited the school nurse two or three times a week and is often sent home with "stomach aches." He's missed ten days of school in the past six weeks. After Devon's pediatrician determines he's physically healthy, Mom is advised by the school psychologist to devise a behavioral contract for Devon to resume regular school attendance.

With the help of the school psychologist, Mom constructs a contract in the Distraction mode. You'll recall discipline in the Distraction mode offers a child two or more rewards for two or more acceptable right behavioral choices. The rewards are chosen to overpower Devon's motivation to stay home. Devon is anticipating the "reward" of staying home from school with Mom. He's doing this because he fears something happening to Mom like it did to Dad.

The psychologist suggests offering Devon a choice to stay with Mom in the nurse's office in school during school hours, a reward which is as acceptable and as appealing to Devon as his misdirected goal of staying home. However, another, bigger reward will also be offered for Devon if he chooses *not* to spend time with Mom in school, though she will wait for him in the nurse's office. Keeping in mind the overwhelming power of Superaffection as a consequence of right behavior, Devon's reward to ignore Mom's presence in school and remain in class is a weekend trip with Mom to a special event, such as a visit to an amusement park.

Here's how a contract could be constructed in the Diversion mode:

Mom arranges a schedule with the school nurse, spanning three weeks. During the first week, Mom arranges to be in the nurse's office at the school between 10:00 a.m. and Noon for the five school days; the second week for Monday, Wednesday and Friday and the third week, only on Friday. She advises Devon arrangements have been made for him to leave class and join her there, if he feels he must, but she will be disappointed in him if he chooses to do so. She also advises him going to the amusement park requires him to visit the nurse's office no more than three times the first week, no more than one time the second week and not at all the third week.

A written contract is given to Devon spanning the three weeks. He is to carry it with him in school. The contract lays out the number of acceptable visits to the nurse's office each week and a pamphlet from the park is stapled to the bottom. After visiting the nurse's office twice the first week and assuring himself Mom is there, Devon is successfully able to remain in class the second and third weeks.

Another set of rewards for Devon's behavioral contract in the Distraction mode might utilize the same visitation arrangement for Mom, but substitute the reward of a video game CD or DVD (without the player) for incomplete compliance with the required number of days in class and the CD or DVD with its video player for total compliance.

Usually, school refusal is an issue which once resolved doesn't recur. However, if it were to recur, and for any form of ongoing defiance, behavioral contracting can be modified to offer what I call "Rewards That "Eat." Here's how they work:

Behavioral Contracting using Rewards that Eat

Imagine several weeks after successfully remaining in class, Devon reverts to visiting the school nurse's office several times a week. Once again, Mom constructs a Behavioral Contract, but now uses a Reward that Eats.

Devon is advised he may earn a cell phone if he is able to remain in class for three weeks without visiting the school nurse during class hours. His three weeks of compliance will restart from any day he "breaks" and visits the nurse during class hours. During those three weeks, however, he may visit the nurse at lunchtime without penalty and speak briefly with Mom by phone from the nurse's office.

When Devon has remained in class for three weeks without a break, he gets a cell phone. A cell phone is a Reward That Eats because someone has to keep paying a monthly connection charge. Devon is advised after he gets his cell phone he must pay 1/30th of the monthly charge (from his allowance or savings, if he has either) for any day he misses class. If he has no money, the phone is disconnected from service that month. These details are written down to avoid any misunderstandings.

Here are other Rewards that Eat:

- •Devices connected to the Internet

- •Devices requiring downloads

- •Devices requiring CD's or DVD's

- •Devices requiring electrical connections

- •Devices with periodic service charges

- •Activities requiring someone to drive to a location

Another form of Behavioral Contracting I call "Constructing the Whole". Here's an example:

Behavioral Contracting to Construct the Whole

Most adults have learned early in their careers complex and satisfying goals usually require persistent effort over time. This is not well understood by many children, but it's easy to teach.

Imagine Johnny, age ten-years, wants his own computer. Now he uses his older brother's machine, but only on his brother's schedule.

Johnny's bedroom looks like a garbage dump. Getting him to put toys and clothes where they belong is a constant struggle for his parents. They decide to devise a Behavioral Contract to Construct the Whole.

Johnny is given a stack of cards with (the same) two items listed each day followed by a space for a check mark. Item #1 is: Put all dirty clothes in the hamper_____. Item #2 is: Put away your toys_____.

At bedtime each night Johnny must give a card to Mom or Dad with a checkmark next to each item, indicating he's completed the task. The cards are collected and counted. When Johnny has seven sequential cards completed, detailing his successful completion of these two tasks for an uninterrupted week, the contract specifies he gets a computer mouse. When he has fourteen sequential days, he gets a computer keyboard. Twenty-eight sequential days earns the monitor and forty-two days earns the CPU.

Since computers are Rewards That Eat, the contract can also detail a "disconnect" consequence for failure to continue to perform these chores.

Before we finish, let's take a look at a couple of forms of moderate defiance bordering on severe misbehavior and some effective techniques to control them.

Techniques to Control Biting, Head-banging or Hair-pulling

Biting

Young children (eighteen-months to three-years) who bite others may have underlying conditions triggering anger or defensiveness (like Bipolar Disorder or Autistic Spectrum Disorders) or impulsivity (like ADHD), but the act of biting is always an inappropriate choice. This means there's always a willful component to biting and the decision to bite can be controlled by appropriate discipline.

An effective way to control biting is to visit a toy store and purchase a cheap, unpadded (that is, *uncomfortable*) plastic football helmet with mouth visor and a tight snap-on strap (difficult for a child to remove). It's not necessary to say anything when it is snapped into place after a biting episode. The helmet "speaks" for itself in the Brick Wall mode. It achieves two goals at once; it provides an uncomfortable consequence for the perpetrator and it protects potential victims. The helmet should stay in place for a sufficient time for a child to become unhappy with its presence and recognize

Alan M. Davick, M.D.

it as a punishment, perhaps 30-minutes. Future episodes typically respond to the mere appearance of the helmet.

Head banging

Head banging is usually due to an underlying physical or mental health condition. The significance of head banging can range from a variation of normal development which will be outgrown, to a symptom of very abnormal development (as with Mental Retardation or Rett Syndrome).

Since children do not engage in hardwired misbehavior by choice, the use of a helmet must be focused on preventing injury rather than discipline. The use of a helmet for head banging is quite effective for the limited purpose of avoiding injury to the child. A helmet used for head banging should be comfortable and well padded.

Hair pulling

Like head banging, hair pulling is usually a symptom of an underlying condition and as such is not solely amenable to the imposition of discipline. If the scalp is the target of the hair pulling, a helmet will be effective while it is worn. To the extent hair pulling has become a habit rather than a symptom of an underlying disorder, the habit can gradually be extinguished by using the combination of a helmet and flexible elbow splints (like plastic toy shin splints with Velcro binders) to limit elbow flexibility and access to the hair.

Since the helmet and elbow splints are likely to be viewed by children as "punishments" for conditions over which they have little or no direct control, these devices should be presented as a path to rewards in the Distraction mode using either Star Charts or Behavioral Contracts to structure their use.

For example, if twelve-year-old Alicia pulls her hair at night, she may be engaged in a Behavioral Contract with a Reward That Eats in the Divergence mode in which, if she agrees to wear a helmet at night for a month, she can earn a cell phone. If she elects to use the helmet with elbow restraints, her parents might pay for half the

ce fee. If she succeeds in controlling the hair pulling
with regrowth of her hair, her parents might agree to pay the entire
monthly service fee. As with all contracts, the details are written out
to avoid confusion or misunderstanding.

As you can see, Star Charts and Behavioral Contracts are limited
only by a parent's imagination. These techniques teach children
compliance with reasonable rules is rewarded, perseverance is
required for bigger rewards and unpleasant consequences follow
defiance. They offer opportunities for parents to engage in the
HoNoR Role by responding Honestly to children's behavioral
choices, offering Nurturance in the form of love at all times and
doling out (Super)affection when it is deserved. At all times,
children are held Responsible for the consequences of their acts.

36

Suggested Reading

1.Managing Misbehavior in Kids: The Mis/Kidding Process; A. Davick; 2014

2.Setting Limits with Your Strong-Willed Child: Eliminating Conflict; R.J. Mackenzie; 2011

3.Toddler ABC Guide to Discipline: Quick Secrets to Loving Guidance: M. Smith, R. Chandler; 2010

4.1-2-3 Magic: Effective Discipline for Children 2-12; T. Phelan; 2010

5.The Happiest Toddler on the Block: How to Eliminate Tantrums; H. Karp; 2008

6.Positive Discipline: The First Three Years; J. Nelson, C. Erwin, R.A. Duffy; 2007

7.Parenting with Love and Logic; F. Cline, J. Fay; 2006

8.Love and Logic Magic for Early Childhood: Practical Parenting From Birth to Six Years; C. Fay; 2000

About the Author

Dr. Alan Davick, a Developmental-Behavioral Pediatrician, has taught parents and professional colleagues how to recognize and manage complex misbehavior in children for 40 years.

Trained at the Johns Hopkins Medical Institutions, Dr. Davick has maintained clinical practice throughout those years. He has, as a Major in the Army Medical Corps, served as Pediatrician-in-Chief at Tuttle Army Health Clinic, Savannah GA and later, while engaged in private Pediatric practice, as Behavioral- Developmental Consultant to the Chatsworth School for Exceptional Children, in Baltimore County, MD.

Dr. Davick has focused his knowledge and experience on separating innate conditions like ADHD, Bipolar Disorder, Cerebral Palsy, Developmental Delay and Epilepsy, masquerading as willful misbehavior, from truly willful misconduct, like Oppositional-Defiant Disorder and Conduct Disorders.

In this book, Dr. Davick teaches you to recognize and ignore merely annoying misbehavior, how to STOP life-endangering misbehavior and how to control willful misbehavior with effective discipline. If you're a parent, you'll learn how to use powerful discipline without going to jail.

Dr. Davick lives with his wife, Barbara, in Cape Coral, FL.

Ordering Information

For more information about Dr. Davick's books, please send your queries to:

Alan M. Davick, M.D.
MISKIDDING, LLC
P.O. Box 101127
Cape Coral, FL 33910-1127

URL: www.DrDavick.com
Blog: www.MisbehaviorInKids.com

See additional books by Dr. Davick at several online booksellers.

Alan M. Davick, M.D.

www.ingramcontent.com/pod-product-compliance
Lightning Source LLC
Chambersburg PA
CBHW050349280326
41933CB00010BA/1393